HORSE PROFILING

The Secret to Motivating
Equine Athletes

HORSE PROFILING

The Secret to Motivating Equine Athletes

Using Emotional Conformation, Behavioral Genetics,
and Herd Dynamics to Choose Training Methods,
Improve Performance, and Hone Competitive Strategy

Kerry Thomas

with Calvin Carter

Foreword by Lester J. Buckley

TRAFALGAR SQUARE
North Pomfret, Vermont

First published in 2012 by
Trafalgar Square Books
North Pomfret, Vermont 05053

Printed in China

Disclaimer of Liability
The authors and publisher shall have neither liability nor responsibility to any
person or entity with respect to any loss or damage caused or alleged to be
caused directly or indirectly by the information contained in this book. While
the book is as accurate as the authors can make it, there may be errors,
omissions, and inaccuracies.

Trafalgar Square Books encourages the use of approved safety helmets in all
equestrian sports and activities.

Library of Congress Cataloging-in-Publication Data
Thomas, Kerry, 1968-
  Horse profiling : the secret to motivating equine athletes / Kerry Thomas with
Calvin L. Carter.
      p. cm.
  Includes index.
    ISBN 978-1-57076-508-7 (hardback)
1. Horses--Training. 2. Horses--Breeding. 3. Horses--Behavior. I. Carter,
Calvin L. II. Title.
 SF287.T47 2012
 636.1--dc23
                        2011050045

Book design by Lauryl Eddlemon
Cover design by RM Didier
Typefaces: Minion, Myriad

10 9 8 7 6 5 4 3 2 1

Dedication

For my mother and father,
Kay and Ken Thomas, for providing me with
the courage and foundation as a child that
allow me to reach forward as a man.

" **My first contact with Kerry Thomas** was near the end of 2011, and it seems a little surreal for me to contribute even so few words as these to his book. Indeed, in view of the scope and depth of the book's content, I find it a humbling experience, for while I have been involved with horses most of my life I am neither an 'expert' nor a 'professional' rider, trainer, or breeder. I am simply a lover of horses who has had the great good fortune to observe and work with them and to be caretaker of some rare and wonderful bloodlines of the Arabian horse, in particular.

"Over time, I have had some enlightening and life-changing glimpses into the enormous contribution horses make to the world of humans. These contributions range from the physical to the more subtle and spiritual—from illuminating a gloomy day with their beauty, to lifting one's spirit with a perfectly timed snort of understanding in one's ear; from some antic clearly expressing their sense of humor and restoring a sense of proportion to one's world view, to hours of incredible tolerance, patience, and empathy that can result in miraculous 'openings' to the world around us for children with special needs or on the autism spectrum. Sadly, in the present day, many horses are more exploited than respected; more used than loved; more an extension of human ego than appreciated for their true worth.

"The idea of 'Natural Horsemanship' has become very popular, but it is also translated by different people into quite different things. Much of it may still be used to achieve fast results at the expense of the horse's mental (if not physical) well-being. That is why Kerry's work is so very timely. There is a real thirst for 'better ways' to work with horses, but many people are not willing to compromise on results. Work such as Kerry's that addresses getting results while still putting the horse first—a holistic approach between mind and body, spirit and science (which, contrary to common belief, do not need to clash!), and where the word 'natural' means just that—is much needed at this time. I am sure that this book will be an eye-opener for many, and I pray that it fulfills its promise and contributes toward bringing horses and humans together in ever more successful and fulfilling ways."

—HRH Princess Alia al Hussein / Princess Alia Foundation

Contents

Foreword

Lester Buckley in Germany with State Premium Westphalian mare Califania.
Photo courtesy of Gero Buesselman.

You may wonder why a student of Natural Horsemanship is writing a foreword for this particular book. Working with the whole horse, inside and out, has enabled me to travel worldwide and lay the training foundation for horses in many different disciplines, as well as help horses with training and behavior problems. From untouched horses in the remote Canadian mountains to top-notch competitive Trakehner stallions in Europe, as I have trained and supervised the training of over 2,000 horses over many years, the principles of Natural Horsemanship have proven out time and again. Living a quiet life with horses out of the mainstream has allowed me time to begin to understand the horse—but this is a journey that I am still on.

I believe William Steinkraus said it best in his foreword to Gustav Steinbrecht's *The Gymnasium of the Horse:* "A horse is a horse and a rider a rider, *the insights of the great trainers are all largely inter-disciplinary,* and applicable to almost anything on four legs once the concepts are understood."

It is, therefore, a privilege and honor to write a foreword for Kerry Thomas' book *Horse Profiling.* I first met Kerry in the fall of 2008. We formed a fast friendship—he had just lost his horse, Geronimo, and we talked about what it is like to lose a horse that you are that close to. He shared some poetry he had written about Geronimo, and I knew that we had a kinship.

Since our first meeting, Kerry and I have discussed at length ways of achieving a better understanding of both the equine athlete and companion horse. In the beginning I was intrigued by Kerry's method, as it seemed to be a fresh and "whole" approach. As humans we can better understand things if we can actually measure them, it is part of our nature. A minute as opposed to an hour, an hour as opposed to a day, a foot to a yard, and a yard to a furlong. (Secretariat probably did more with minutes and furlongs than any other horse in sport that I know.) The wonderful thing that Kerry has done for serious students of the horse is to provide a way of *measuring* dimensions of the horse that we only had a "gut" feeling about in the past. Certainly this kind of "sixth sense" has been well developed by a rare handful of horsemen—seasoned horsemen who have a real sensitivity for understanding all aspects that make up a horse and his mind, body, and spirit. Now, thanks to Kerry's insightful research, we can all actually begin to understand and measure, if necessary, the mind, emotions, and "spirit" of the horse—what makes him "tick" beyond simple physical athleticism.

The ideas Kerry shares in this book apply to all disciplines and all horses. Understanding the nature of the horse is really the key to unlocking his total potential, whether he is a racehorse, dressage horse, jumper, event horse, Western performance horse, trail companion, or your partner for ranch work. I grew up in the ranching culture in Texas where horses were used for work. A fascination with the nature of the horse led me from the back roads of Texas cattle ranches to a college education that focused on a study of the horse, then on to a successful career working with National Cutting Horse Association Open World Champion and Hall of Fame trainer Willie Richardson. I have worked for some of the largest ranches in the world, including the King Ranch in Texas and the Parker Ranch in Hawaii, and studied Natural Horsemanship with the "Father of Imprinting," Dr. Robert Miller. Always intrigued with the precision of dressage and jumping, the opportunity opened by invitation to study and ride in Germany, and I achieved riding performance medals in dressage and sport jumping, as well as my "Trainers C" License in both disciplines. That experience led me to achieve two dreams: training with top classical riders, and breeding (hopefully) sound, emotionally stable stars for the future of horse sport—part of what I now pursue alongside my wife, Mary, on our farm in Hawaii.

When breeding and training sport horses, there always seems to be a few select horses that come along that are special, but not necessarily "easy." These horses usually tend to either frustrate us or lead us to dig a little deeper into what's causing the miscommunication or problem. Oftentimes we see moments of brilliance only for the horse to later "fall through the cracks."

It was Alois Podhajsky who reminded us not to forget to thank the difficult horse, for he often teaches us the most. In Kerry's work we have the means to "see inside" this "misfit," and by providing training based on the specific needs of the horse, achieve wonderful results. This insight not only lends itself to helping the misfits, but allows us to better serve the sound, stable equine partners we work with and enrich their lives, as well.

Sometimes we tend to work with our horses with a predetermined agenda, perhaps because it has worked the majority of the time for us in the past. Kerry's work equips us with the information we need to compose a specific training program for each individual horse based on that horse's individual makeup. I think this is especially important with horses that tend to be stalled and are limited in interaction with other horses and their "herd"—something that applies to many of the top performance horses in the world today.

This book can help you learn to fulfill the complete needs of your horse by addressing the aspects of his training and care that are most often overlooked. There are many fine books written on proper feeding and nutrition, as well as numerous how-to manuals on training for almost all disciplines. But I believe *thoughtful students of the horse* should have this work in their library, as well, as a complementary, and even necessary, core reference.

I am excited for Kerry, as well as for you, the reader, to share this journey. I look forward to a future in which we can work together to really make a difference in the horse world.

Lester J. Buckley
Kailua Kona, Hawaii
www.buckleysporthorses.com

Acknowledgments

From Kerry

I would like to offer my thanks and appreciation to the many people who helped make this book a reality, having given so freely of their time and efforts whenever anything came up that had to be done yesterday! Thank you to Calvin Carter for helping me take my raw research material and craft it into book form. Thanks to "The Closer" Pete Denk for helping at the eleventh hour. Larry Knepper, my trusted and dear friend—you do so much for me and THT quietly behind the scenes… your efforts are always appreciated. To Gillian Vallis, who so willingly opened her Pine Knoll Farm to me on many occasions during this process. Thank you for the help and support of Tonia Fenstermaker, Barb and Mike Grosso, Jim Rittenhouse, Steve Barger, Duane Miller, Joe Vineski, and I cannot thank Lester Buckley enough for penning the Foreword. And a big thanks goes out to the Trafalgar Square Books team, too.

There are so many people, places, and horses I owe so much to—they've enabled me to not tell you in this book *what I know,* but indeed to share in this book *what I have learned so far.*

From Calvin

It has been an honor and a pleasure working with Kerry Thomas. Thank you, Kerry, for guiding me on my journey into the intimate drama of life in the Equine Circle.

Thanks to my good friend Larry Knepper for his encouragement and support.

Special thanks to my wife, Lois Haywood, whose friendship, love, and encouragement have made the journey a joy.

1 Introduction to My Philosophies and What Lies Ahead

"It was a natural process, a natural journey of discovery of the equine, and my own self."

I wish to take a moment to thank you for reading my book; I hope you enjoy what, for me, is the culmination of an eclectic-style research that, as time went by, began to focus on the intimate drama of life in what I call the "Equine Circle"—a kind of society with rules and hierarchies serving to keep order and, ultimately, the survival of the equine species. I consider myself an "equine investigator"—a researcher who develops specific protocols based on a study of the psychology and *Emergent Properties,* or the potentially hidden qualities that can come forth during the life experience of a horse. (I'm going to talk more about these things, in detail, in the pages to come.)

How I Got Here

I think that growing up in Southern Pennsylvania had a lot to do with my love for the horse (fig. 1.1). These magnificent creatures have always had a special hold on my heart and the bond traces to early childhood, as far back as I can remember. My earliest memory of a horse is like a photograph in time. My father, a carpenter by trade, took me to a nearby barn where horses were stalled. Dad held me in his arms as we looked at the horses. One curious sort reached out to nip at me. A rather dubious first memory—I smile upon it now.

1.1 Growing up in rural Pennsylvania greatly influenced my desire to study and learn all that I could about the magnificent horse. Here I am with Ade, my favorite Friesian.

I found the blend of human and horse life flourishing around me on neighboring farms and fields to be something unique and intriguing. I especially enjoyed watching the Pennsylvania Amish work the fields with their team of draft horses and the families cantering down the road in their horse and buggy (figs. 1.2 A–C). Local steeplechases, flat racing, and the area farms, barns, and people who worked with horses all greatly influenced my desire to learn as much as I could about the equine world. Even then, the thing that stuck with me most was the way the horse always seemed to fit so nicely into his surroundings.

In my early teens, the study of all animal life, especially the horse, was my passion, and that desire to investigate and discover compels me to this day. I always

1.2 A–C Throughout Pennsylvania there are numerous horse farms and Amish communities. The sight of an Amish horse and buggy cantering down a rural road, or an Amish farmer plowing his field with draft horses, always captured my full attention.

quietly dreamed of someday working with horses, to share in the interesting and, to me, yet-to-be discovered world of the horse—the herd. My desire to know as much as possible about the horse eventually led me to the Bighorn Mountains in 1989 to study the behavior of wild Mustangs in their natural habitat (figs. 1.3 A & B). When I look back, it seems like a long journey before arriving at the place where I knew that the key to understanding and knowing the horse was found in his *Emotional Conformation.* Yet, it was a natural process, a natural journey of discovery of the equine, and my own self. Indeed, it was a journey that eventually delivered me to my *emergent self*—my mind developing beyond that of its physical boundaries, accruing self-awareness and independent thought.

The Birth of the Thomas Herding Technique

My study of the wild Mustang led to the creation of the Thomas Herding Technique (www.thomasherdingtechnique.com) and the development of the *Emotional Conformation Profile,* which is a tool I use to analyze horse behavior. Each horse has a unique personality, but it is the *Emergent Properties*—hidden potential found within the horse—that eventually reveal his true potential. *Behavior triggers* and *behavioral overcompensation* can be tremendous barriers, but they can be overcome with the help of an Emotional Conformation Profile. This form of "horse profiling" helps the horse owner develop specific training protocols that enable the horse to perform his very best.

1.3 A & B In 1989, I took my first trip to the Bighorn Mountains in Wyoming to study the behavior of the wild Mustang. Little did I know that my first encounter with the Mustang would change my life forever. My research and study there led to the creation of my Emotional Conformation Profile, which is a tool I use to evaluate horse behavior (see p. 55).

The Thomas Herding Technique (THT) has already helped horse owners and trainers in Europe, South America, Australia, and Hong Kong, as well as in the United States, discover the hidden potential of their equine athletes. In addition, THT is slated to work closely with developing programs all over the globe. Our research at THT and interest in providing educational outlets, as well as services for specific horses and programs, continues to expand. For example, THT provides seminars and lectures for corporations looking to improve their communication outreach. (I call these programs "Translating the Herd Dynamics of Communication"—you can find out more on my website: www.thomasherdingtechnique.com.)

As you turn each page in this book, I hope you will begin to see a clear picture of my journey. By sharing my personal "awakening" to the world of the equine and my own resulting self-awareness, it is my sincere hope that you will find esoteric *Emergent Properties* hidden within yourself, as well. In my study of the Equine Circle and the horse, I see a reflection of man. I have little doubt that ongoing research into the behavioral, social, and overall psychological aspects of the horse will continue to reveal more about humankind. Researching another species and making discoveries that are applicable for the enhancement of man is not a new concept. There is much to be gained in the collateral information uncovered, even if the investigative nature is not one of physical manifestation. The horse is not a lab rat in a maze, or a mouse to be used in testing medicinal reactions. But, more than any other animal, the equine has been the enabler of man's evolutionary march forward through time. Thus, the horse is indirectly a reflection of human development. That being the case, there is much that can be discovered within the Emergent Properties that cross the boundaries separating the two species.

The impact of the mind over the body, in its various forms and levels of reason and thought, is the driving force behind the advancement of a species. Physical evolution does not start simply with change alone because it is responding to the conceptual aspect of a decision based on an environmental necessity; in essence, this is survival in the horse and creativity in the human. Simply put, without a reason, the body will not react. This is life, the connective tissue, the very fiber that allows for the drive forward. This is also a truth that embraces all living things. Evolution takes place with every decision made. Thus, the key to breeding and training the equine athlete lies not in the focus on the physical specimen as the controller, but nurturing that which drives the horse forward.

It is within the creation of individual training protocols that the door opens to a *crossover concept,* in which *mental preparedness* allows for *optimum physical*

1.4 A–C Throughout history, equine and human athletes, such as Seabiscuit, Jesse Owens, and Jim Thorpe tapped into their inner hidden potential to overcome tremendous obstacles and become a champion.

performance. Once you establish the focus and agility of an athlete's mental ability, human or equine, you can nurture that into physical conditioning, and thus enhance and advance the potential hidden within the athlete. To measure that hidden potential, I developed what I call the *P-Type* (see p. 82) as the indicator of those Emergent Properties. The mind is the *vehicle* of survival for the horse. Any evolution or improvements in the physical condition of the horse always originates from a decision of the mind. The difference in achievement often comes in the gray area that lies between changing the focus from pure, physical training, to that of mental training to advance to the next level.

What Separates the Great from the Mediocre

Training the horse for physical conditioning is training for mediocrity. So it also is in breeding the horse only for physical conformation. In focusing only on the physical, you may have to breed and train an extreme number of horses in order to get one miracle horse that will make your career. If ten horses do not bring you success, you breed ten more—and so on and so forth. The result of this breeding and training program produces a surplus of would-be equine athletes.

Real athletic training involves the act of training the mind to control and influence the body. The difference between success and failure, excellence and mediocrity, often comes down to *the mental capacity of the athlete to focus on a given task*. Athletes who possess that mental capacity to focus are able to utilize their hidden Emergent Properties, as well as every piece of physical power and talent, thus controlling every aspect of their physical ability. Not only is that often the difference between professional success and failure, but happiness and sadness as well. History is full of athletes—human and equine—who tapped into their hidden Emergent Properties to achieve fame and glory. Olympic champions Jim Thorpe and Jesse Owens, as well as baseball great Jackie Robinson, had to overcome racial prejudice to become successful in the sports arena. Champion Thoroughbred Seabiscuit had to overcome emotional and physical barriers in order to become one of the greatest racehorses of the twentieth century (figs. 1.4 A–C, and see more about this in chapter 10, p. 157).

You've heard this expression before: "He (or she) has *so much potential*." Realizing one's potential is the act of those Emergent Properties coming to fruition, becoming reality. The converse effect of not realizing one's potential is suppression. Once suppression is in place, mediocrity becomes acceptable, and far too often it is seen as success, when so much is yet untapped—in both human and equine athlete alike. Suppression of one's potential is bad, and it can lead to many problems, including disease and mental disorders, as I'll examine in chapter 9 (see p. 125). In such a case, the Equine Circle is broken.

On the Discovery Trail

By nature, the horse is a wild herd animal and over the centuries man has tried to breed that characteristic out of the horse. To a certain extent, man has tamed the horse. Try as we might, though, we will never fully succeed because the wild nature, the herding instinct *(basic instinct)* is the very mechanism that Mother Nature has built into the horse for survival.

Thus we have the paradox of an animal, wild by nature, living in an artificial, domestic environment created by man. How to understand the horse and care for his well-being will be the subject of this book. On the pages ahead, we will look at the following:

- In chapter 2 (p. 13) we will examine instinct and behavior and the influence they have on the horse in the Equine Circle.

- Building trust in the horse is important to all training. In chapter 3 (p. 27) we will look at the artificial, domestic environment and how to enter into the Equine Circle.

- The environment is the foundation for healthy living. In chapter 4 (p. 35) we will look at how nurturing the *Natural Herd Dynamic* in an artificial, domestic environment has an impact on equine behavior and is vitally important for the physical and emotional well-being of the horse.

- In chapter 5 (p. 55) we will look at *Emotional Conformation Profiling* and the important role it plays in breeding and buying equine athletes.

- In chapter 6 (p. 77) we will take a more detailed look at Emotional Conformation Profiling in order to determine how it can promote the physical and mental well-being of equine athletes and help them reach their maximum potential.

- In chapter 7 (p. 89) we will examine the questions: "What is a 'Communicated' Equine?" And then, "How do we apply that knowledge to our training program?"

- Smooth transitions and patterns of motion are important for both the show horse and racehorse to be a successful competitor. In chapter 8 (p. 105), we'll look at training the equine athlete with these conditions in mind.

- *Potential Withholds* and *Equine Mental Illness* are tremendous barriers preventing the horse from living to his fullest potential. In chapter 9 (p. 125) we will look at several case studies outlining those conditions.

- In chapter 10 (p. 157), we'll look at a special case study and see how embracing the magic within the spirit of the horse and nurturing the Natural Herd Dynamic helped a famous racehorse overcome the physical and mental barriers that initially prevented him from becoming a success.

As we move forward in our discovery of the equine, and hopefully, those Emergent Properties hidden within ourselves, it is my wish that we continue to seek what I consider "the magic within the horse…a view from the hoof."

1.5 A & B There is magic within the spirit of the horse… a magic that captures our heart and enthralls us…a magic that entices us with his speed and power.

Locating the Magic Within

Often mystical is the nature and flowing beauty of the horse. For centuries mankind has been enticed by the allure, infatuated with the power, and awed by the magic within the spirit of the horse (figs. 1.5 A & B).

Intertwined along the path of life, through many trials, wars, and mass migrations, the human spirit so often has been lifted and propelled by its partnership with the horse. Indeed, prior to modern society, the horse is the stoic and tireless companion that has been a part of nearly every major human movement, war, or sporting event our species has ever undertaken. Try to imagine the human race and evolution of societies without the horse. Our world would be much different. More than any other creature on earth, the horse has been our best friend and companion.

For many in our society, the history of the horse and his partnership with us through the ages is unknown or forgotten. Ask your average horse owner, horse lover or enthusiast, how horses made their first trip across the ocean to America or about the migration paths of breeds into the new world. Ask him or her if there is an "endangered list" for breeds of horses. Ask the average racing fan questions about the history of the Thoroughbred, and he or she will probably have few, if any, answers.

We see the ever-so-expensive accoutrements and trappings, and we marvel at the many breeds we have bred—all the wonderful horses: the speed on the racetrack; the dancelike moves of dressage; the height of the jump; the precision of reining; and the poetry of cutting. It is worth marveling at for sure but pales in comparison to the accomplishments the

1.6 A–G For centuries, the horse has been man's constant companion. He has enabled us to explore new worlds and defend old ones.

horse has made in the past: the war horse that helped shape great nations; the big, strong, athlete that plowed the fields for our crops; the incredible endurance of the horse that carried forth humanity onto the prairie and hauled the cannon across miles of land to forge new worlds and new governments, or to sustain the old (figs. 1.6 A–G).

It isn't the image of a loping Western pleasure horse, the extended trot of a Warmblood, or the speed of a Thoroughbred on the racetrack that most enthralls us. It is the spirit flaming bright inside each horse that makes him special. Indeed, not only is it this beautiful spirit and grace alone that makes the horse so precious, but also the valor in which the horse stood by us as we moved along our journey of human evolution.

When visiting a battlefield such as Gettysburg, I see the memorials for the great men who fought and died and know that alongside many of them was a trusty horse. Like so many angels, the horse was a refuge of power and safety, a spirited beast standing

1.6 A-G *continued* The horse has hauled heavy loads and harvested our crops.

beside the soul of man, there to guide and assist him in the heat of battle. I see the horse as a true, living-and-breathing monument in the field of history. Touching the horse is like touching the past. Many generations before us have heard the same sounds, recognized the same smells and all of the characteristics that make up the "magic" of the horse. For me, this connection is a direct link, a window into the past, a way to touch a small part of the world that was familiar to times gone by— and it reminds me who we are and how we came to be at this moment in time.

Connecting Spiritually....Connecting Physically

The horse is not a pet, though it seems easier to assume so. An animal, especially one that has taken such great care of us so many times in the past, deserves to be respected and treated as a companion. If you love your horse, or all horses, as many of us do, it behooves you to appreciate the history of the equine.

Horse and man share what could be called a spiritual connection. Horses, more than most any other animal, offer all of us an interactive relationship without limits or prejudices. The magic in their large, soft, eyes is full of expression and curiosity, and they seem as interested in us and the things we are doing, as we are of them—true signs of companionship.

In my work with horses, I have had the opportunity to socialize them to interact with people, mostly children, afflicted with various physical and mental challenges. The senses of both the horse and child connect to reach far beyond the physical expressions we are accustomed to, breaking boundaries we never knew existed, and offering unspoken and enchanting interactions between child and equine that can bring tears to your eyes. In this fleeting mo-

1.6 A-G *continued*
He has entertained us with his speed and athletic prowess.

1.6 A-G *continued* He has carried us over obstacles, big and small.

ment of time, there is a feeling of deep spiritual connection with the horse. Connecting spiritually is paramount to connecting physically, for the spiritual connection is the higher power that transcends and controls all that follows. The horse today may not be needed as much for pushing forth human evolution, but the cathartic nature of his presence will never be out of season.

Throughout the ages we have looked to the horse to entertain and help us with tasks both spectacular and mundane. Today, the horse is looking to us for help. Inhumane slaughter and wild lands picked clean of the magnificent Mustang are just a few of the problems that plague the equine community. Is this how living monuments to human history are to be treated?

What the domesticated horse needs most from us today is to be understood and properly taken care of on the farm, on the racetrack, and in the competitive arena. If we wish to return the full measure of what the horse has given us, we need to reach beyond our own world and consider how best to enable him to be all he can be.

2 Instinct and Behavior in the Equine Circle

"Acquired instinct is combined with basic instinct to enable survival."

The first step in embracing the magic within the spirit of the horse is to gain a clear understanding of how the horse fits into the herd, or what I refer to as the *Equine Circle,* which I described in chapter 1 as a kind of society with rules and hierarchies serving to keep order and, ultimately, the survival of the equine species. The makeup of that society can be likened to a puzzle, and each individual horse is like a puzzle piece. Each puzzle piece is important to complete the puzzle, just as each individual horse is necessary to have a herd. Recognizing and comprehending the *circle* of equine reality is the first part of this journey. The second step is to interpret the processes that occur within the Equine Circle.

Natural Herd Dynamic

By nature the horse is a herding animal. The Natural Herd Dynamic is the everyday behavior and interaction that occurs within the intricate social order of the Equine Circle (herd), and the only way to gain an understanding of the structure and complexities within this circle is through an open-minded observation of the horse (I'll talk more about social order in chapter 7—see p. 94). Whether a band of two horses or a band of six, there are social and communicated dynamics within that circle that change little from group to group. Traveling down a farm lane and looking at horses in a pasture, you are likely to see much the same behavior that you would if you were observing a herd of wild horses (figs. 2.1 A & B).

2.1 A & B When you study a typical family group of wild mustangs, such as the ones shown here from my time in Wyoming (A), you can discover a lot about the makeup of the herd. The stallion just left the vicinity, and the lead mare (bay, upper left corner) is investigating droppings to determine how long ago the stallion was there, as well as if any other stallions have visited the spot. The adjunct mare (top right, in the scrub oak) is standing in observation of a mid-level mare (gray) and her yearling (bay, lying down). Traveling down a farm lane in Kentucky viewing horses, you will see much the same behavior as you would in the wild (B).

The key to understanding the makeup of the Natural Herd Dynamic is found within herd communication, and how all members work in unison for one goal: herd survival. Three natural stimuli—the environment, sensory, and voice—influence the Natural Herd Dynamic.

- *Environmental influences* are one of the three main keys of the Natural Herd Dynamic. A reaction by a single horse to a change in the environment is quickly communicated to all herd members who, in turn, quickly respond to the same stimulus. This ability to quickly communicate environmental influences allows for two things: survival, of course, and learning. The weanling learns as much from the reactions of his mother and family group to stimuli as he does via self-discovery. This is a vital piece of the fabric of herd life and keeps the young members safe.

- The senses of sight, hearing, smell, taste, and touch are the sensory aspects of interpreting and communicating environmental influences to the rest of the herd. Learned, or *acquired behavioral triggers,* such as the sight or smell of wolves or a bear, will trigger a certain response, much like the smell of rain in the air or a grassland area. Horses inform and teach one another via their communication every day, and in a natural setting these tools of learning are reflective of their daily lives and the needs therein for survival. The ability of a horse to learn and develop good sensory skills is key for survival because a proper interpretation of changes in the environment allows the horse to react to those changes while not drawing attention.

- Horses, indeed, voice their opinions and feelings, and each horse has his own distinctive voice. There are several layers to a horse's voice—it is a language of tones, pitches, and lengths. Greetings to one another come in various forms, as do locating calls, or "find me" calls. Calls that communicate stress, danger, emotions, and health all play a part in the herd's "voice" and are important elements of the Natural Herd Dynamic necessary for survival.

From the influence of those three stimuli, two survival instincts emerge: the *basic instinct* and the *acquired instinct.*

Basic Instinct

The *basic instinct* has two governing bodies: sensory and voice parameters. Its elemental purposes and constructs are obvious: survival, procreation, drinking, eating, sleeping, and all of the life-giving dynamics that make a horse, a horse. The *Sensory Horse* is the equine in control of the moment-to-moment influx of information and the translation of it—for example, breeding behavior, the fly that lands on the back, or the taste of good or bad food, to name just a few.

Voice is also an important basic key necessary for survival, as communication in a society is paramount to its success. The transfer of information allows for the Equine Circle to function in an ever-changing world. Just consider the march of ants along a jungle floor or the swarming of birds and bees, and you can see how important communication is to *any* society.

Smell, touch, posture, and *sound* are the sensory and voice parameters the horse relies on for survival in the Equine Circle. Equine body language is often accentuated by sound; the voice works in conjunction with the body.

Acquired Instinct and Associative Learning

The *acquired instinct* is governed by only one dynamic and that is the environment. The environment is the world of the Equine Circle and the life experience of the horse in that circle—the circumstances, objects, or conditions that surround him. It provides the many *triggers* that allow for *associative learning* and control *associative memories* (see below). Acquired instinct is combined with basic instinct to enable survival, and it is developed from the string of associative memories related to the horse's life experience.

Associative learning, in which a new response is associated with a particular stimulus (trigger), is developed from the environmental stimuli received by the horse. Anything penetrating the circle is associated as a trigger mechanism—something that affects associative learning, and therefore, survival of the horse. What the trigger is initially associated with, and the memories it creates, determines how it is interpreted by the horse in the future (see further discussion of triggers beginning on p. 19).

We can use trigger mechanisms as a training tool. I was given a case of a racehorse who had a lot of issues with the starting gate. The work I did with him included removing him from the racetrack environment—I took him to a cornfield, growing high with corn. Why? Picture yourself standing in a cornfield row. It is a closed space left to right, you can only see for a distance in one direction, and you can feel things rubbing against you on each side. The cornfield mimicked the starting gate, without triggering the same response in the horse. Therein lies the key to associated stimulus training techniques.

The acquired instinct, in essence, serves as the control factor of the basic instinct, which is why it is developed as the horse matures. This is also called *adaptability.* Fitting into the environment as that environment changes is a powerful but basic survival dynamic.

In nature, the law of evolution dictates that an animal *without* an acquired instinct is a food source that eventually is apt to be replaced, whereas, a species like the equine *with* an acquired instinct is, indeed, moving forward in the game of survival. The basic instinct and the acquired instinct blend together in such a way that has allowed the horse and the Equine Circle to live and evolve for many years. As a result, the horse is well equipped, physically and mentally, for his life in nature.

2.2 A & B When the foal is born, he has every basic instinct he needs for survival. The mare "jumpstarts" the foal, encouraging him to "wake up" to the world around.

Individual Horse Personality

From the dynamic of acquired instinct is birthed the *Individual Horse Personality (IHP),* which is developed by the associative memory of the horse. The Individual Horse Personality is essential not only for surviving but learning how to fit in the hierarchy of the Equine Circle. Each horse must find his place within the circle, and the Individual Horse Personality plays a major role in accomplishing that.

The Individual Horse Personality is comprised of many influencing factors and coexists with the acquired instinct. These two dynamics influence one another and together serve as a monitor of the basic instinct. Even though much of the Individual Horse Personality stems from the components of the acquired instinct, individualism is equally as powerful from the onset, so much so that it can become *its own* trigger mechanism—this being the individual horse propensities. These *propensities* (intense natural inclinations) are blended from traits given the horse by his sire and dam, and from the experiences that stem from the basic dynamics of the acquired instinct. It is within this behavioral dynamic that tendencies can become "normal" behaviors that often are natural for the horse, yet are sometimes envisioned by humans as problems or issues.

2.3 The first six months are crucial for the development of the young horse. During this period, everyday life experiences build the foundation of the acquired instinct the young horse will need to not only survive but to thrive.

Kerry's Corner

Question:

I have always found interesting the concept of triggers, habits, bad behavior, and even the consideration of variable degrees/forms of "addiction" in horses, so-to-speak. I was wondering then, what your point of view might be in regards to these things? Are there any analogous parts of the whole from the horse that can be related to people and in training human athletes?
—Carter, Indiana, United States

Answer:

Something to always keep in mind when *triggers* (p. 19) are in play is that triggers come in two forms. The first form is that of a *direct trigger*. This results in a behavioral response, good or bad that stems from a direct influence or stimulus, either environmental or otherwise. For example: the smell of roses is pleasing to me, like the smell of grain or fresh grass is to the horse, and leads to a smile in me as the grain perhaps inspires a nicker on the part of the horse. The more powerful form of trigger is the *associated trigger*—when a reaction comes not from a direct act or stimulus but from some form of stimuli that has been *associated with* an act. This leads to a potentially unstable platform but if handled correctly based upon the individual, can be used to train the horse or indeed any athlete forward, and is often thought of as "anticipation" or "expectance."

Once anticipation is in place, the horse can become in a way *addicted* to the feeling and quite dependent upon it because he or she cannot move into the next place or moment in time until this assimilated dependency is satisfied. This makes it quite important to continually advance the horse's mental training through variable stimuli and associations to get the desired outcome. To help prevent the athlete from being *too conditioned* and assuage bad behavioral issues down the road before they are, in effect, *institutionalized*, it is important to introduce variable training stimuli because the horse is incapable of knowing the difference between *habit* and *addiction*.

When an associated trigger is comprehended *collectively* by two

The Role of Instinct and Behavior Triggers in Equine Development

When a foal is born, he has every basic instinct he needs for immediate survival; otherwise, he would stand little chance in the wild as a prey animal (figs. 2.2 A & B). The foal also has a capacity for learning so that not only does he survive, but he thrives to become part of the next generation of smarter, better horses. Learning provides for survival of the fittest.

At a very early age, the foal's acquired instinct takes over from the basic instinct and the foal begins his journey of learning and discovery with the environment as his teacher (fig. 2.3). Acquired instinct is formed as the result of a very dependable associative learning dynamic: *When I did this, this happened. So, therefore, whenever I do this, that should happen.* Which translates to: *The mountain lion came at me and I ran. So, therefore, if he comes at me again, I will run again.*

or more of the senses, it is *not* in danger of being an *emergent addiction.* Dependency or addiction takes over when *one* sense is depended upon for the comprehension of the whole. We often see addiction issues come to light in former equine athletes who find themselves in new environments and new homes. Horses can be quite dangerous to good, new owners when, from out of nowhere (it seems), very bad behavior related to associated dependencies and trigger addictions appears.

To treat such cases, it takes time and patience and an investigation to find out what is really influencing the situation, real or imaginary. It is important to remember that, in my opinion,

addiction is not itself tangible; instead it is manifested in the form of anticipation. When anticipation occurs, it begins to take over control of *reaction* more and more, and these are the roots of bad behavior. This is why you cannot simply treat bad behavior by the removal of one thing without filling it with another; open voids in life are "missing pieces of the puzzle"—and when voids appear, both humans and horses will fill them. When voids *are not* filled, you've created the foundation for Equine Mental Illness (see p. 125). Proper treatment of bad behavior in the horse requires the exact same *nurturing* philosophy as does properly training the equine athlete. It is my opinion that addiction is the act of filling in the

pieces of the puzzle with arbitrary things that are temporary, mentally controlling the sense of sustainability.

It is important to know that there is a difference between *consistency* and *addictive repetition.* You *do* want to be consistent in achieving your desired result with your horse, but you also want to have a well-balanced and adjusted horse who reacts equally as well, even when there are variable degrees to the overall approach you are using. An emotionally sound horse is a horse with good *mental agility,* making adjustments "on the hoof" without becoming befuddled in the process. From human to horse, to be successful we must all learn to win, from within.

For associative learning to have merit, it must have the quality of immediate stimulus reaction, which means: *Tell me once, I live. Tell me twice, I may not.* Equines do not have the evolutionary luxury of hesitation. Ask, then run, isn't a very efficient survival technique for a prey animal. Because of this, the horse's ability to reason is limited at best, and it is controlled by associative memory and not by actual "thought," as we understand it. Associative learning is nature's byproduct of the basic instinct foundation. *Running from danger* is the basic instinct dynamic, *recognizing or sensing the danger,* is the acquired instinct dynamic. In other words, running is, of course, natural. Knowing when to run is learned. If this were not the case, the horse would be running away from everything, all day long.

Of course, if the horse could not learn, he would not survive in the wild. But learning comes in two parts so that a distinction can be made between life-threatening circumstances and harmless events. Out of this necessity comes the associative learning and memory that is controlled by the difference-maker—the *trigger.*

Behavior Triggers

The *trigger* (stimulus) allows the horse to recognize the difference between what he should fear and harmless life experiences. The trigger is the mechanism from which a new experience is introduced, and it can be anything, great or small. Once this new piece of information is introduced, it becomes associated with the surrounding or ensuing events. Once it is learned, it becomes an associative memory (figs. 2.4 A–D). A couple of good examples of triggers come to us from the late Federico

2.4 A–D This mare is heading into a new environment as she is led toward the chute to the back walking ring at the Keeneland November Breeding Stock Sale in Lexington, Kentucky (A).

New environments initiate behavioral triggers. Without the luxury of reason, a horse always will react with caution, erring on the side of self-preservation. The mare's walker tries to lead her into the chute, but she is not convinced it is safe—note her head position, ears, and eyes (B).

Tesio, an internationally renowned Italian owner, breeder, and trainer of Thoroughbred racehorses (see more about Tesio on p. 52). From 1898 until his death in 1954, Tesio bred racehorses at his Dormello horse farm near Dormelletto, Italy, and during his lifetime the farm produced numerous classic champion Thoroughbreds. In his book, *Breeding the Racehorse* (J.A. Allen, 1994), Tesio tells a story about a feverish foal with an abscess that was treated by a veterinarian wearing a white coat. The veterinarian did not use an anesthetic when he lanced the abscess. After treatment, the foal recovered and returned to the Equine Circle, for the most part happy and content. However, from then on, whenever the foal saw anyone wearing a white coat, he would run and try to hide.

In another example Tesio tells the story of a group of racehorses that were stabled near a racetrack. The racetrack had a bell that rang at the start of each race. At feeding time, if the horses heard the racetrack bell they became so excited they would go off their feed.

The association of the white coat or the racetrack bell became triggers of unwanted or bad behavior resulting in stress and discomfort for the foal and stabled horses. Anything within the horse's circle, large or small, even people or events that seem to have nothing to do with the horse, can have a profound effect on his behavior. Recognizing those triggers is crucial for the handler to enable the horse to live in comfortable, stress-free environment.

Identifying triggers of behavior can be likened to putting the pieces of a puzzle together. In a natural environment, the basic instinct and acquired instinct

2.4 A–D *continued* This is a pivotal moment. We as humans may know a situation is safe, but the horse's reactions are guided by instinct. When a horse is at the crossroads of "fight or flight," as shown here, the human handler must remain calm and confident (C).

Triggered by the confident demeanor of her handler, the mare enters the chute and relaxes (D).

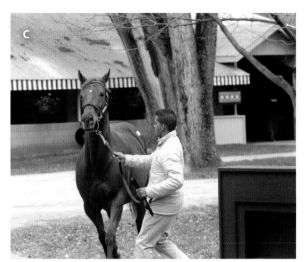

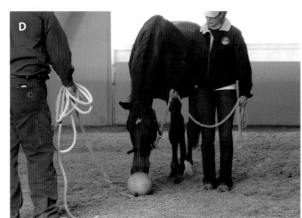

2.5 A–E Assimilated Imprinting allows horses to learn tasks and function efficiently in new environments. Here I am working with Sophie, a Thoroughbred-Oldenburg cross, at the Pine Knoll Center for Integrated Horsemanship in Lexington, Kentucky. Allowing Sophie to walk to the ball encourages her to assimilate to an object—animate or inanimate—while in motion (A). Sophie identifies the new object in her environment (B). Proper decision-making while in motion can be a life-or-death situation in the wild. In the sport horse's world, it leads to more efficient performance. Sophie investigates and processes what the object is, then reaches the ball and accepts it in her environment (C & D). The lesson learned is that when something new enters her line of sight, she does not need to be overly reactive. You want your horse to be confident, not afraid, when investigating new objects. Here, the object is targeted, identified, and finally released (E). The physical speed at which this test is performed is not relevant.

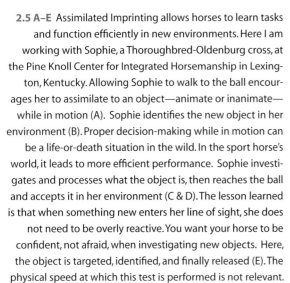

provide triggers of behavior formed by environmental settings. For example, the cry of a mountain lion and howl of a wolf are signals for the horse to run from danger. However, in a domestic environment, the pieces of the equine puzzle do not fit so neatly together because of the human presence in the environment. The threat from a mountain lion or wolf is nonexistent; thus, triggers of behavior are completely different than those learned by a horse in the wild. The feverish foal with the abscess did not have any fear of the man in the white coat *until* the man in the white coat lanced the abscess without applying an anesthetic. In the wild, the foal could run from perceived danger, but the domesticated horse is completely dependent on man for his safety and comfort. When that trust is betrayed resulting in stress and discomfort, "reentering" the now "broken" Equine Circle takes time and patience on the part of the handler.

Assimilated Imprinting

Associative memories enable the horse to piece together the puzzle of the Equine Circle. If we study the mystery of the equine puzzle, we find that the foundation of environmental growth is what I call *Assimilated Imprinting,* which is the integration of new triggers to old associative memories. Assimilated Imprinting is the purest form of learning, and it is the foundation for adaptability, which translates into survival.

A prey animal will retain a strong basic instinct dynamic and keep a close hold on the associative memories that have contributed to his survival. For the horse to be adaptable, he must have the ability to override associative memories with new ones overlapping the old via the introduction of new triggers and stimuli. Being able to adapt and therefore survive as a species shows us that even as the horse grows, he can be socialized to new environs. This socialization is done through the equine's ability to assimilate.

Overriding associative memories by using Assimilated Imprinting is possible because of the generally friendly, gregarious, and curious nature of the horse (figs. 2.5 A–E). The feverish foal can be taught to no longer fear the veterinarian in the white coat if his handler wears a white coat during the daily routine of feeding and taking care of the horse. Over time, with patience and careful handling, the foal soon learns a new lesson involving the person in the white coat.

One might ask: "Why go to all the trouble? Wouldn't it be easier to have the veterinarian remove the white coat when taking care of the foal?" Yes, perhaps it would, but the trigger of unwanted behavior still remains in the associative memory of the foal, and you don't want it to "re-fire" years down the road when the foal is grown and about to compete in an upper level dressage test, begin a reining pattern in a major futurity, or run in the most important race of his life. Unresolved triggers of bad behavior can have a profound impact on the horse, resulting in issues such as anxiety during competition, jigging or shying in the warm-up ring or paddock, or balking on entering the show pen or starting gate.

Sometimes behavior is not a reaction to a trigger but is merely a tendency or trait of the horse's Individual Horse Personality (see p. 17). The key to knowing the difference between *personality traits* and *triggers* lies in one's ability to recognize the triggers that dictate certain behaviors or cause stress in the horse.

Stress

Stress has a very harmful influence on the domestic horse. And it can be especially harmful for the sport horse and racehorse before a competitive event. Often, it can

Kerry's Corner

Question: **How can I reassure an off-the-track Thoroughbred that racing is done, and he can relax now?**

—Vivian, Kentucky, United States

Answer: This is indeed a good question and obviously one that can be asked over and over again for many a horse changing careers. Removing the horse from one way of life (that may have been stressful), and introducing a lifestyle that allows the horse to actually *be a horse again,* so to speak, can be fraught with many tiny battles within the equine psyche as the process of Assimilated Imprinting takes place (see p. 23). The key to understanding how to find ways to readjust the horse to

a new world first requires you try to view *that* world from the horse's perspective.

Coming off the track is being removed, not from the racetrack as much as from the entirety of the performance horse's *lifestyle,* which he has experienced from day one. The manipulation of environmental influences plays a major part in the proper and successful training of the athlete—as we will discuss at length in this book—and thus it is the proper manipulation of the environment that will work

toward "reeling in" the horse from his former way of life. Among the key things to remember is that the vices you may see the horse with or that he may develop as time goes on in the "new" environment, can be manifestations that combat the stress or boredom that often comes annexed with a *more relaxed environment.* The horse's body may stop its demanding workout schedule easily enough, but the mind still races on, fully developed and assimilated to survival within the confines of the only world it ever knew. The competitive racing world rarely delivers wide open spaces and continual contact with other horses in open, nonstructured settings. Therefore, suddenly be very difficult, if not impossible, to get the horse to relax and settle down. The antics of an agitated Quality Road delayed the start of the 2009 Breeders' Cup Classic for five minutes before he was eventually disqualified from the race (fig. 2.6). The famous classic champion Thoroughbred War Admiral was notorious for becoming anxious before a race. He held up the sixty-third running of the Kentucky Derby for eight-and-one-half minutes. The Preakness Stakes was delayed for three-and-one-half minutes because him, and the Belmont Stakes seven-and-one-half minutes.

Not all stress-related behaviors are expressed by the horse in ways such as I've just described. Hidden stress is the most dangerous, and we often do not know it exists unless a true understanding of the Individual Horse Personality is assessed. Expression of stress is as subject to the equine tendency as is everything else. However, because of the fascinating ability of the horse to adapt to his environment, there is always time to override the associative memory, so long as the trigger stimulus has not been too disturbing. If the basic building blocks of the Individual Horse Personality and acquired instinct lie within the environment, it is within the

springing the "retired" racehorse into a more "natural" venue isn't always as smooth a process as one may think. The horse will naturally acclimate as time goes on because the horse is a survivor and has been gifted the natural ability of Assimilated Imprinting. However, this truth does not necessarily mean that the horse does not need attentive nurturing.

There are essentially three main factors involved in the processing of the equine psyche:

1 Start by creating *mental* stimulus without too many *physical* demands: make the mental portion of stimuli outweigh the physical requirements of task achievement.

2 This leads you into the second stage, which is getting to know your horse's place in the *Herd Dynamic:* how high is the horse "on the totem pole" (see p. 99)?

3 Once you've established the Herd Dynamic, seek to develop *variable* stimuli that are equal to and eventually a challenge for the horse, without necessarily seeking to expand his abilities by leaps and bounds. If the horse is truly retired from his former athletic career but capable of competing in a different sport, that is great—just be sure that a new career befits the established Herd Dynamic. The object of retirement is a *nonaggressive approach to learning new*

things. Remove the timetable, be creative, and don't be afraid to be the horse's "herd buddy" while you introduce him to new friends and new places.

Embedded in the training or retraining of horses is the fact that we often encourage the development of bad behaviors, vices, and recalcitrant outbreaks because we are way off the mark in our comprehension of the Herd Dynamic. for the horse in question. Establishing the level of the horse is the foundation for all that follows. It is the barometer that tells you if you need more, or less, to process the horse and move forward toward new goal achievement.

environment where keys of change can also be discovered.

The Individual Horse Personality includes the *emotions* of the horse, as well as the traits of the sire and dam blended with the tendencies of their offspring. It is the supplementation of the *emotional triggers* (triggers that evoke certain feelings, like fear) that have a lot of control over the seasoned equine's ability or desire to assimilate. Emotion feeds off emotion, making the emotions you see and sense in the horse very powerful, indeed. Fear, elation, anxiety, and stress: these are all part of life experiences in the Equine Circle, and they have a great influence on the physical and emotional health of the horse, and affect his ability to adapt to and perform in new surroundings.

Often, horse owners, riders, and trainers do not know the difference between an expression of the Individual Horse Personality and behavior triggers. They only see the *effect,* not the root *cause.* Should one witness a young horse becoming agitated before the start of the Kentucky Derby, it is logical to assume that the noise of the crowd or the sight of the starting gate and anticipation of the race ahead is the reason for the horse's behavior. But, perhaps it is actually the white windbreaker worn by the gate handler that is the trigger—because long ago, when the horse was a feverish foal with an abscess, he learned to fear anyone wearing a white coat.

Unfortunately, when the horse acts up in such situations, physical restraints, the whip, and will of man, forced on the equine, is sadly most often our solution to the problem. Far too often, treatment for the *effect* is all that is doctored.

The Thomas Herding Technique can help the owner, handler, rider, and trainer identify triggers of bad behavior, as opposed to Individual Horse Personality traits, as well as provide ways to address them, ultimately enabling the horse to live to his fullest potential.

2.6 Quality Road (#12) refused to go into the starting gate before the 2009 Breeders' Cup Classic at Santa Anita Park in Arcadia, California. His stress and agitation only escalated the more the gate crew tried to force their will on such a high-dynamic horse (see p. 99). The hood that was placed over Quality Road's head completely removed one of his senses and added to the chaos.

3 The Artificial, Domestic Environment: Entering the Equine Circle

"Developing a bond of trust with the horse is the first big step
toward embracing the magic that resides within him."

From the work horse to the show horse to the racehorse, all breeds of domestic horses are dependent on man for their well-being. Most owners take good care of their horses, providing them with the best food, healthcare, and shelter possible. But, unfortunately, it frequently is the environment *we* have lovingly created for the horse that is directly responsible for many of the behavioral and metabolic disorders we are trying to treat and cure. Landscaped farms, well maintained barns, and expensive tack do look nice, but in reality those trappings are more for our own benefit and have little to do with the welfare of the horse—he is more concerned with eating, sleeping, breeding, and the freedom to "just be a horse." Given a choice between a warm dry stall and steady meals, and living in the elements, whatever the hardship, the horse's preference would almost always be freedom to roam and graze in the wild.

In the natural environment, acquired instinct and associative learning (which we discussed in chapter 2) are obtained by the horse interacting within the Equine Circle. The same is true for a horse's associative learning in an artificial, domesticated environment. When we remove the horse from the natural world he is specifically equipped to live in, only the environment has been changed—not the animal's capacity to learn or his method of learning within that environment. *The horse is still a horse* with a basic instinct to roam and graze freely in the wild, though we often treat him as if he is a pet. Therein lies the conflict.

The way a horse is handled, who or what he is exposed to, indeed, every aspect of the *controlled equine world* containing our human element, makes up the environment our horse perceives and experiences, and that dictates his learning. This element of associative learning begins long before any actual *training.* The environment is the foundation of life experience for the horse and is often the trigger of unseen stress and behavior issues we only observe much later (see p. 24). Understanding how the Natural Herd Dynamic works and applying that dynamic in an artificial environment is of utmost importance to the horse owner. Without that understanding, any attempt to interact with the horse will be fraught with frustration.

In this chapter we'll examine the Equine Circle, and in the next, I'll talk more about nurturing the Natural Herd Dynamic in an artificial environment.

The Equine Circle

For the horse in the Equine Circle, there are no long term goals and aspirations— there is only life within the moment of time that the horse is passing through. The horse does not sit in his stall and make plans for the time he will spend in the pasture or show ring. Everything the horse is and will become—the past, the now, and the future—is enveloped within the cycle of singular moments of time that is the world of the Equine Circle. The reality of the moment is all there can be, for this is what allows the horse as a herd animal to exist. The horse needs to stay alive within each moment and be ready to react at all times. Survival is what we call it (fig. 3.1).

The associative memories and associative learning that we have discussed and that make up the acquired instinct operate within the circle, woven and blended with the ever-present basic instinct as a necessity for survival. In nature there may not be a second chance.

3.1 Keen awareness and the ability to react at any moment are integral for the survival of the wild horse.

Herd Hierarchy

As a herd animal, the horse has a natural desire to make friends, not enemies. Herding within the Equine Circle is pure and honest. Although there may be struggles within the herd to maintain and reaffirm the hierarchy, this does not include preconceived plans or subterfuge. Having a friendly, peaceful relationship within the herd perpetuates safety (fig. 3.2). Safety is comfort. The horse is *not*

comfortable when there is stress and anxiety within the herd. (I discuss herd social structure in more depth beginning on p. 94.)

As we touched on in chapter 2, the horse is equipped with incredible senses that he relies on for survival. In a pasture, the Equine Circle will be as far-reaching as the ears can hear, the eyes can see, and the nose can smell. It can be as close as the fly on the horse's back, but this fluctuates, depending on the survival requirements of the moment.

3.2 As a herd animal, the horse has a natural desire to make friends and perpetuate his own safety.

Entering the Equine Circle

Developing a bond of trust with the horse is the first big step toward embracing the magic that resides within him. Without that trust, that emotional and physical connection, all work with the horse will be in vain. Anything entering the Equine Circle is instantly scrutinized. Assessing any possible threat is the horse's first order

3.3 A–H At the Pine Knoll Center for Integrated Horsemanship, I prepare to enter the circle of a bachelor herd comprised of two males—a pony named Domino and a Thoroughbred-Oldenburg cross named Shane (A).

When entering the Equine Circle, it is important to take nothing with you that the horse could view as threatening. When threatened, the horse will do anything to survive. I clear my mind and note my posture, and the way I carry my head and hands. The calm demeanor of Domino, contrasted with the reaction of Shane (in the background), reveals that Domino is the most dominant in this herd (B).

Once the leader is identified, I make my intentions clear to the one in charge by turning toward him (C).

of business, especially when a human is involved. Your demeanor, the way you bear yourself from day to day—expressions, attitudes, postures—is scrutinized by the horse before he allows you "in."

Often people enter an Equine Circle, and then they think that because they were there once, they can go again whenever and however they choose. Every time you approach a herd of horses, it is like the *first time.* They identify you and identify your intentions all over again, every time you return, whether it is five times a day, once a week, or once a year. Horses live moment by moment. They may recognize you and become accustomed to reading your intentions, but they are always investigating you. You just might not know it.

It is also important to remember that your horse is not required to enter *your* circle in order to survive, though he may wish to be close to you. Make no mistake, when your horse approaches, *you are the guest* in the circle of the horse, and human rules of life are circumvented by the horse's acquired instinct for survival. The horse will seek signs of danger first and react accordingly.

How you enter this circle has a tremendous impact on future training and handling of the horse (figs. 3.3 A–H). How you communicate with the horse is extremely important—communication controls all aspects of equine life, including movement, stress or anxiety, and comfort (see more about this beginning on p. 89).

Control Your Emotions

The way you communicate your desires to the horse should *never* be threatening. The horse is not "out to get you," and he does not plot to "get even." It is, therefore, important to always be in control of your own emotions when entering the Equine Circle—your emotions dictate how you communicate and interact with the horse.

When you feel yourself enter the circle with a negative frame of mind or in a manner that could be seen by the horse as threatening, break away from the circle and reenter at a later time—even just a few minutes later can make a difference. Stay positive.

3.3 A–H *continued* Making a connection with the horse and establishing trust is the goal of entering the equine circle, so I make myself smaller as I approach and casually establish my position close enough to Domino to gain acceptance (D & E).

I make a connection with Domino, but his buddy Shane tries to get me to react to his threatening posture (F).

Avoid any body language that could be perceived as a threat, such as raising your hands, walking fast, or walking directly into the face of a horse. A horse doesn't care if you have to run to catch an airplane or make it home in time for dinner, and so these things should *not* be a part of your frame of mind. Remove your agenda from your approach and simply allow yourself to be "absorbed" into the herd.

Clear Your Mind

The best way to enter the circle is to take nothing with you that will confuse the horse or make him anxious. Remember you are being scrutinized for any signs of danger. Everything you do communicates something to your horse.

The positive or negative stimulus the horse acquires from you as you enter his circle forms powerful triggers (see p. 19) that later manifest as what is interpreted (by humans) to be good or bad behavior. Any bad behavior you observe in the horse should be handled with understanding and patience. The horse is only behaving in a manner that is determined by the life experience or associative memory learned from the acquired instinct, and it will take time and patience to eliminate those triggers of bad behavior.

When your approach is not threatening, when your mind is clear, the horse will allow you into his circle. However, if the horse feels threatened, he will do whatever is necessary for survival.

Make a Connection

When you successfully enter the circle, a true connection with the horse is possible. The dynamics of my form of *Light Touch Therapy (LTT)* lie within this very moment, for "channeling" and communication with the horse is enabled by the connection of emotional sensations to physical ones (figs. 3.4 A–C). Light Touch Therapy is a stress-relief program designed to center the horse's focus to your every move and intention even before you make it. Physically, it amounts to very light stimulation designed to send powerful im-

3.3 A–H *continued* Once you've made the connection, you have a trusted friend—Domino, as the more dominant of the two horses, continues to graze and Shane, seeing this, appears more at ease with my presence and eventually joins his pal (G & H). At this point I have established myself within the Equine Circle and can begin a training program with them.

pulses between nerve and muscle while centering the equine focus through mental stimulation and breathing—the latter manipulates the way the horse's brain interprets the physical stimuli. This elevates the horse's capacity to not only interpret your touch but to translate it emotionally, decompressing emotional stress beyond the physical result.

Light Touch Therapy is a process that expands and improves a horse's ability to interpret stimulus within his space, and therefore it can be very useful for a horse with close space infraction issues, such as particular sensitivity to touching certain parts of his body. You can try LTT for yourself:

1 Touch the horse all over his body until the horse is comfortable to the feeling and doesn't react to your touch with body language (for example, turning his head). This indicates he is beginning to *interpret* the stimuli rather than simply react.

2 Next you want him to begin to interpret the *intention* of your touch. Remain in the horse's space, but slowly pull your hand away, first by only inches, then progressively further, up to a foot away. Then repeat in reverse, gradually returning your hand to his body for additional light touches all over his body.

3 The horse will begin to *interpret you,* whether you are touching him or not. When the horse ceases to react to your *actual* touch and *intended* touch with body language, you have succeeded. The horse's habit of automatically associating close space infractions with danger should begin to fade away. (Important note: if

3.4 A–C My form of Light Touch Therapy (LTT) is a stress-relieving technique and an internal focus exercise for horses with close space issues, among others. It is also a good way to "make a connection" upon entering the Equine Circle. Here I touch Shane, pull back a little, and then resume touching him in a different area of his body (A & B).

3.4 A–C *continued* I want Shane to get used to me touching him and being in his space. This helps the horse recognize stimuli around his body and space in a safe, comfortable setting. You want your horse to be able to interpret things without becoming agitated. I also want Shane to use his senses to consider what I am doing, rather than simply re-acting with body language, so we exchange breath (C).

The goal is to lengthen the time of LTT application each time you do it. You want your horse to concentrate on what you are doing in his space until you decide to end the exercise. When the horse breaks focus, don't go back in. Revisit the exercise another time.

the horse continually tries to move away from you or repeatedly turns his head to see what you are doing, stop the exercise and resume another day.)

Small Amounts, Short Sessions

The best way to introduce the horse to new stimuli is in small amounts that are fol-lowed by times of rest. Therefore, one has a much greater impact by working with the horse for short consistent periods followed by periods of relaxation. When you work a horse hard and don't allow for periods of rest, you will do double-work for half-results.

The equine schedule and the typical competitive horse's training schedule are far removed from one another. The horse learns well in the herd environment, and he has survived a very long time because of it. Spending all day entering and exiting the circle at intervals, and introducing new training stimuli as you do, is the most natural "herding technique" there is.

Using the Power of the Equine Circle in Training the Sport Horse

Establishing an efficient line of communication with your horse allows for more efficient training protocols. Once you have been welcomed into the Equine Circle, you can use *Natural Herd Dynamics* in your training (see p. 99). You are operating on *the horse's* level. Of course, once "in" the circle it is important to reflect the com-

munication dynamic of the horse you are working with. If you are working with a high level horse, use slight body language and intentions as your primary com-munication. If you are with an "underling" horse that uses a lot of body language, you may have to use more body language of your own to get your point across. You are the coach, the teacher, and you must understand your student. We further explore the Equine Circle and herd hierarchy in chapter 7, beginning on p. 89.

Nurturing the Natural Herd Dynamic in an Artificial, Domestic Environment

"I…mainly ascribe my success to the principles of keeping my mares on the move. That's the natural way." —Federico Tesio

Now that you have entered the Equine Circle, the next step in your journey is to nurture the Natural Herd Dynamic in an artificial, domestic environment by making farm life and its surroundings as natural as possible for your horse. Nurturing the Natural Herd Dynamic is a big part of embracing the magic with the spirit of the horse, and it will go a long way in warding off many of what I call *Potential Withholds* and *Equine Mental Illnesses* that I discuss later in this book (see chapter 9, p. 125).

If you have experienced a power outage for an extended period of time, you know how frustrating and stressful it can be when your normal everyday environment has been changed or altered. The same is true for the horse in a domestic environment. Although the modern day horse, to some extent, has been "tamed" by man, as a species the horse is a creature with a basic instinct to roam and graze free in the wild. When his freedom is restricted, as it is in a domestic environment, stress can develop that has a profound effect on your horse and other horses in his "herd." Rough play in yearlings, agitated impatience in mature horses, and an overall tension in the herd can be seen and felt. The usurping of food and water sources and the order of the herd hierarchy can become greatly obscured and makes an otherwise orderly group seem anything but—and if it affects the group, it affects the individual. This is a natural reaction to unnatural circumstances.

Creating as natural an environment as possible—and allowing the equine athlete to inhabit it—goes a long way to nurturing the Natural Herd Dynamic I introduced you to on p. 13. This promotes the emotional and physical well-being of your horse. The socially content, happy equine harbors a reduced stress rate and convalesces better, if not faster, when ill or injured. These are important characteristics for a top competitor.

Creating a Natural Environment

4.1 Nurturing the Natural Herd Dynamic in an artificial, domestic environment will go a long way in promoting the physical and emotional well-being of the horses in your stable. Like their cousins in the wild, the domestic horse has the same basic instinct to roam and graze freely in open pastures.

The environment—the circumstances or conditions that surround you—is the foundation of healthy living, and the ideal goal for the equine athlete is to create a horse-friendly, domestic environment with settings as close to nature as possible. The horse has evolved masterfully in order to live successfully in the wild. When man domesticated the horse and removed him from his natural environment, the only things that changed were where the horse got his food, water, and shelter. The horse still has a basic instinct to roam and graze, but in the domesticated present,

that freedom of movement is restricted and the horse is dependent on man for his well-being (fig. 4.1).

As equine caretakers, it is our responsibility to understand how the domestic environment affects the horse on all levels—physical and mental. As a social animal, the horse depends on daily interaction for mental growth. Striking a balance between the physical environment and the emotional requirement of the horse to survive within that environment is essential. For survival, the horse has to be physically and mentally flexible to live in changing environments. Horses can do this because of their social structure and mental aptitude to *acquire* layers of experiences that essentially are memories. This *Emotional Conformation* of the horse—how his psyche is built—guides him through life and helps him grow and adapt as necessary. (We'll take a closer look at the topic of Emotional Conformation in chapter 5, beginning on p. 55.)

The *ideal* scenario of fresh water, open space with room to roam and run, good grass, ample sunshine, other pasturemates (preferably a "herd"), and accessible cover promotes both physical and emotional health. This atmosphere feeds the horses' senses, enriches their body and mind, and improves performance—a proper herd environment being so vital to learning. As we all know, however, reality is often much different. Few are fortunate enough to have a lot of grazing land with clean, fresh, running water so they can turn their horses out to pasture regularly. However, when your acreage is limited, your herd is small, and there is no water source, it is still possible to establish a daily regimen of *Mental Stimulus Exercises* (see p. 43) in order to keep your horse or horses in good health.

Whether you have a small budget or millions at your disposal there are certain basic steps you can take to make farm life harmonious for the horse. The main thing to keep in mind when nurturing the Natural Herd Dynamic in the artificial environment is that in addition to the *physical needs* of the horse, any plans or designs for structures, paddocks, and pastures should also take into consideration his *emotional needs*. Much has already been written about how to properly care for the physical needs of horses by other authors, and I won't rehash that information here. But, I would like to note the highlights I believe are keys to promoting the mental health of the horses in your stable.

Allow for Freedom of Movement

Barns are for people, pastures are for horses. Freedom of herd movement is one of the most important elements in nurturing the Natural Herd Dynamic in a domestic environment, and it serves three main purposes: it helps to establish the herd hierarchy of the Equine Circle (when herdmates are included—see p. 40), it is a major component of natural stress dissemination, and it keeps the physical systems of the horse in working order. Turning your horses out to pasture as much as possible, for as long as possible, will go a long way to promote their physical and emotional needs.

The more acreage you have for your horse to roam and graze in the company of others, the better. However, realistically, some farms don't have a lot of grazing land. I recommend at least one acre per horse for the proper nurturing of the Natural Herd Dynamic.

Especially in the case of mares and foals, turning horses out from May to October for the majority of their hours—as long as there is good shelter for them during bad weather—enables them to receive the beneficial nurturing that is so vital for good physical and mental health. Short periods in mild weather during the winter months will provide the physical and mental stimulation so necessary for good equine health.

For equine athletes in training, it is vital to include as much "free time" in paddocks during training breaks as possible. Even little bits of time outside are valuable for the emotional wellness of your horse. Twenty minutes of sunshine is better than zero. Think of how you feel when cooped up inside all day.

Turnout Establishes Herd Hierarchy

In the wild, the Equine Circle is sustained by the proper order of horses fitting together in the herd like the pieces of a puzzle. However, in the domestic environment, the puzzle pieces of the Equine Circle do not fit so neatly together—primarily because horses are so often solitary, confined to stalls, and freedom of herd movement is restricted. Freedom of movement and pasture companions are essential for the proper establishment of the herd hierarchy (see p. 94). The horse, not being a forward-thinking, reasoning animal, can be easily stressed when any piece of the herd puzzle does not fit or is missing.

Turnout Reduces Stress

The way in which the horse deals with stress is a built-in basic instinct designed to handle the demands of nature. The equine basic instinct (see p. 15) is equipped for many things, but confinement is not one of them.

The buildup of stress for horses who are, for the most part, sheltered and raised in stalls, can be just as dangerous and deadly as the rattlesnake and mountain lion are to the horse in the wild. This is also greatly compounded when the added anxiety of injury is incurred. The convalescing horse is faced with immeasurable anxiety and stress, with even less avenue for its dissemination.

The smaller the space, the higher the stress. Horses confined in stalls can suffer from what I call Equine Cabin Fever (see p. 147), and this condition is highly unfavorable to the healing process. Lack of attention to this detail can have a catastrophic impact on the future emotional well-being of the patient. Even after the horse is healed, the emotional scarring within can be a *Potential Withhold*—anything of a physical, but mostly mental, nature that restricts the horse and prevents him from living up to his fullest potential (see p. 125)—times ten. Every experience in the Equine Circle is layered one on top of another upon the basic instinct dynamic, clouding the processes the horse uses to learn and assimilate.

Turnout Keeps the Physical Systems in Working Order

When you think of the equine as a flight-based species, you know that, without a doubt, *movement* is the primary point of power and vital to survival. A study of equine anatomy introduces you to a plethora of bones, ligaments, bursa sacks, tendons, muscles, and joints, all designed to work in unison, and at great speed when necessary. The hoof itself is an amazing design in form and function. Yet we see innumerable lamenesses, unsoundnesses, and hoof-related issues in our domestic horses (the most horrific being laminitis).

However, if you study wild horse herds in various parts of the United States, from the Spanish Mustangs living in the rugged, steep environment of Wyoming and Montana to the tough ponies roaming the sandy, swampy terrain of the Eastern Seaboard, you would be hard-pressed to find the same frequency of leg- and foot-related problems that are prevalent in horses living in the domestic environment.

Consider the surfaces that the horse walks on in the artificial environment— generally flat, mostly solid surfaces—and you may find a clue to the etiology of leg and hoof issues. The array of surfaces traversed continually in the wild, hard to soft, steep to flat, rocks, trees, shrubs, and mud, are all important natural strength training tools for the horse. This constant movement over a variety of terrain assures that as the horse grows, the myriad working parts of the leg and hoof anatomy are exercised and doing the work they were designed to perform. The end result is a rugged, sturdy animal. Wild horses live in a world where their "gym workout" is meted out every day, while the artificial environment is often very confining. Without facing the same demands of nature, the leg anatomy of the domestic horse is far more likely to suffer injury.

Allow for Formation of a Herd

The number of horses in a herd can vary and to a great extent is dependent upon the amount of land that is available for the proper nurturing of the Natural Herd Dynamic. Herd size is also case-specific because of the differences between *Individual Herd Dynamics* of males and *Group Herd Dynamics* of females (see p. 99).

A natural bachelor herd in the wild can consist of as few as two stallions or colts and contain as many as six or seven. But the reality is that male horses "buddy-up" with one or sometimes two other (male) horses, so even when you see seven males grazing in a bachelor herd setting, each horse maintains close relationships with only one or two others in the herd. Mares and fillies are the main body of the herd structure and generally have the majority influence, and thus three to four fillies or mares will be together at all times.

4.2 When a horse is identified as a "loner" and does not interact with other horses, it is time for the owner to take an active role communicating with that horse in order to ensure his continued mental growth.

The bottom line is, many horse owners do not have the luxury of having more than two horses together at a given time. Two horses are better than one in order to promote the beneficial nurturing of the Natural Herd Dynamic. If you can only afford one horse, it is a good idea to provide him with companionship in the form of other animals, such as sheep, goats, chickens, or ducks.

The Lone Ranger

The loner, standoffish horse who does not participate and interact with the herd presents unique challenges for the horse owner and requires special handling. If a horse would rather eat alone in a stall instead of out in a paddock or pasture with other horses, he may be getting the nutritional requirements necessary for good physical health, but he is missing out on the social and mental stimulus of interacting with other horses "at the dinner table," so to speak. Social skills, hierarchy issues, and enhanced communication ability are all collateral positive side effects, emotionally and mentally, that occur in this situation. When a horse stands off from the herd and does not participate in feeding or interacting with the other horses, wedges are added to the social skills and dynamics of the loner, and those wedges create aberrations, which can potentially develop into Equine Mental Illness (see p. 125).

When a loner horse is identified, it is time for the horse owner to take an active role of communicating and interacting with that horse (fig. 4.2). Feeding time is a great opportunity to initiate social interaction with the standoffish, loner horse. If the horse is safe enough to be with in his stall, stand nearby and every once in a while, kick his hay away a bit or pick up some and drop it—make the horse *focus* and *refocus* on you. If you do not feel safe in the stall with the horse, stand just outside, and do what you can every so often to take your horse's focus off his food long enough to note your presence and *manage it,* even if it's just locating you with the twitch of an ear.

More than any other horse in the herd, the loner horse is completely dependent on the horse owner to provide for his physical and emotional needs. Nurturing the Natural Herd Dynamic of the loner horse can be especially challenging as it is up to the human handler to provide the stimulus and social interaction necessary for the development of good mental health. It is not enough to ride your horse every few days and think he has received the stimulation he requires. This kind of interaction is good in that it provides your horse the physical exercise he regularly needs, but it does not place enough social demands on the horse to enable him to become an active participant in the herd—even if the "herd" is just the two of you.

You need, in short, to make time to *talk to your horse* by implementing Mental Stimulus Exercises that challenge the loner horse on a daily basis (see more on this on p. 43). Spend time together doing nothing but interacting and communicating without a physical requirement. Moving in and out your horse's space is an excellent example of a Mental Stimulus Exercise that requires your horse to communicate with you, without your actually moving, leading, or riding the horse. Such exercises help nurture the important characteristics that make your horse a "complete" horse, and eventually he should be able to join and interact with other horses in a herd.

Allow for Spacious Barns and Stalls
The saying goes "more is better," and while not always true, it *is* true for larger horse breeding and training farms. While barn number and size depends on your pocketbook and the size of your herd, ideally you should have a separate barn for mares, a

4.3 Spacious barns and plentiful pasture are ideal for the domestic horse. Even with a limited budget, you should strive to allow enough outdoor space and outdoor time to nurture the physical and mental growth of the horse. The social needs of the equine should also be considered, and the formation of a herd encouraged.

barn for mares with foals, a barn for stallions, and another for weanlings and yearlings. Each barn should have its own paddock or paddocks so the horses within can go in and out of the barn freely, or at the very least on a daily basis (fig. 4.3). When a property has multiple barns, they should be located as far away from each other, and the caretaker's quarters, as possible in order to prevent the spread of infectious diseases.

Stalls or boxes should serve as necessary homes for the horses only when they are in training, laid up due to injury, or during periods of bad weather. The stalls should be spacious with plenty of room—two horses of like size should be able to

stand head to tail. At a minimum, a stall should be one-and-a-half the total body length of the horse within it. In addition, barns and stalls should be well ventilated and allow in natural light.

Establish a Daily Regimen of Mental Stimulus Exercises

Horses in the wild experience a wide range of challenges on a daily basis. Those challenges develop and strengthen physical and mental health, which is vital to herd survival. Much like his cousins in the wild, the domestic horse needs to be physically and mentally challenged on a daily basis in order to promote good health. A daily regimen of Mental Stimulus Exercises is one of the easiest things to develop and implement, and it is an important element in nurturing the Natural Herd Dynamic of the horses in your stable.

Make Feeding Time Interesting

I've mentioned before that feeding time is a great opportunity to employ a Mental Stimulus Exercise that makes some *natural environmental social demands* on the horses in your artificial, domesticated environment. Horses in the wild are constantly on the move from feeding grounds and watering holes, and in searching for and finding, and traveling to new sources of food and water, they deal with any number of physical and mental challenges. One way to recreate those challenges in the domestic environment is to, on a daily basis, change the location of where you put feed and water. Make your horses *find* their hay and water in the paddock each day. Make them depend on one another and on their senses. It might seem like a lot of work to move your water buckets to different locations each time you turn your horses out, and it might be inconvenient to not drop their hay in the same old spot each day. But your convenience doesn't matter as much as your horse's growth and future ability to learn.

Create a Mental Stimulus Obstacle Course and Paddock

One thing that horse owners can do to nurture the Natural Herd Dynamic in the domestic environment and provide the horse with the necessary mental stimulation to promote good health is to create a *Mental Stimulus Obstacle Course* and a *Mental Stimulus Paddock*. Via the Thomas Herding Technique, both a convalescent pathway and obstacle course can be made available, based on the requirements of the horse and circumstances of the environment. The goal of the Mental Stimulus Obstacle Course and Paddock is to develop the ability of the horse to learn how to make smooth, efficient transitions of motion while maintaining an elevated focus and pace. This is accomplished by allowing the course of natural assimilation to enhance the mental soundness of the horse. The performance horse needs to be able to manage multiple stimuli, and the course and paddock are designed to provide the mental stimulation necessary to promote that ability, whether the horse is at rest or in motion.

The ability to interpret various stimuli smoothly and decisively in motion is the governing factor for just how far your horse can be elevated physically—finding ways to nurture this ability is your key to competitive success. As you've heard me say before, *the mental capacity of the equine controls the physical output of the athlete*, making overall mental preparedness a key ingredient to the "competitive edge." Mental soundness is very often the defining point between success and failure. Physical conformation can fall short or be inconsistent without the congruence of a sound Emotional Conformation (see p. 55).

Both the Mental Stimulus Obstacle Course and the Mental Stimulus Paddock designs can be formatted to fit into many different areas—large and small.

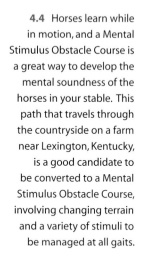

4.4 Horses learn while in motion, and a Mental Stimulus Obstacle Course is a great way to develop the mental soundness of the horses in your stable. This path that travels through the countryside on a farm near Lexington, Kentucky, is a good candidate to be converted to a Mental Stimulus Obstacle Course, involving changing terrain and a variety of stimuli to be managed at all gaits.

Mental Stimulus Obstacle Course

The Mental Stimulus Obstacle Course is a designed pathway of approximately 6 feet wide that travels over variable types of terrain (changing footing, inclines and declines), allowing for multiple mental stimulus interpretative protocols to be employed while the horse is in motion—from the walk, to the trot, and then a relaxed gallop, depending on design, location, and athletic goals (fig. 4.4). Using the natural "lay of the land" is a great way to teach your horse and yet avoid spending too much money on course construction. Hills, water, shrubs—all can be useful tools when training the equine athlete, whatever the discipline.

Ask your horse to move through belly-high grass, rushing creeks, and thickly wooded areas. Let him see deer, birds, and wind-blown leaves. Have him experience weather conditions and surface transitions. The Mental Stimulus Obstacle Course teaches your horse to efficiently interpret stimuli *while* working toward your training goals. The result is a more well-rounded, mentally sound horse.

The obstacle course embraces the concept of *time-in-motion* (see p. 114) and allows for protracted interpretation with a wide array of the key ingredient—interval stimuli training in varying degrees of pace. Horses learn while in motion, they assimilate best when required to *make decisions on the move,* and the obstacle course is designed to help the horse learn how to be focused at all times while interacting and moving within his environment.

Mental Stimulus Paddock

On a smaller scale, the Mental Stimulus Paddock is designed to provide the same type of mental stimulus interpretative protocols found in the obstacle course, but in a contained environment. Basic examples of elements include:

- Incorporate multiple entrances to the paddock—on a daily basis change, how your horse enters and leaves the paddock.

- Move the location of feed and water buckets (as previously mentioned—see p. 43).

- Place small trees or shrubs throughout the paddock. Shrubs should be big enough the horse cannot see around them, forcing the horse to rely on all his senses and forms of communication to ascertain if there is anything on the other side.

- Place small flags at random throughout the paddock, which will be especially effective on windy days. Waving and vibrating objects keep the horse sharp and keen to identify motion while grazing, and they aid in teaching him to manage multiple stimuli without a person nearby.

- Include a "roll area," such as a large sand pit for the horses to roll in.

- Add different types of footing in different areas of the paddock.

Mental Stimulus Exercises for a "Rainy Day"

Horses like the freedom of roaming and grazing in the pasture. When they are confined to the barn because of inclement weather, it is important to continue with

4.5 In the herd environment, the young horse learns the communication and interaction skills he will need later in life. The young horse that is socially sound has a trainable mind—he will learn faster and be a better achiever.

a daily regimen of Mental Stimulus Exercises. One good exercise to employ during bad weather is to use the open aisleway area between the stalls and found in most barns as a walking and exercise "ring." Walk a few laps, communicate with your horse, and add a little mental stimulation to his day, however limited.

Maintain the Family Structure for as Long as Possible

Maintaining the family structure of the mare and foal is an important element in nurturing the Natural Herd Dynamic in the domestic environment. The first six months of life is one of the most formative periods of the foal's existence (fig. 4.5). The bond between the mare and foal is extremely important for the foal's development and survival. During this period, the foal is developing an *Individual Horse Personality* (see p. 17), but he has yet to realize his own identity and place in the herd separate from the mother—that occurs after weaning.

A great deal of study has gone into the concept of "imprinting" newborn foals—extensively handling and grooming the foal at birth to accustom him to his handler. Dr. Robert Miller, a pioneer in the field, noted the benefits of imprinting in his book *Imprint Training of the Newborn Foal* (Western Horseman, 2003). I personally feel that imprinting the foal at birth and during his first six months helps make the weaning process less stressful for the foal. Weaning can be the cause of later performance issues in a horse. Weaning the foal too early or using abrupt "stall weaning"—the practice of leading the mare and foal into a stall and then leading the mare out again while shutting the foal inside—causes a detrimental setback in the foal's behavioral development. (I discuss the trauma of too-early weaning to a greater extent in chapter 9, beginning on p. 127.) In the wild, weaning occurs gradually, as the foal is able to handle and care for himself. The horse owner and breeder should respect this aspect of the Natural Herd Dynamic in the domestic environment.

Manage Sources of Stress

Responsible horsemanship means much more than a treat in the pocket and providing your horse with clean, spacious shelter. It is an effort to create a domestic environment similar to one found in nature. Knowing your horse and understanding how important it is that he properly fit in the puzzle of the Equine Circle will help you to make his environment *a little less artificial* and more natural.

Preventive stress tactics, even for the loner horse who hasn't a friend in the field, can be discovered and implemented. In order to do this properly one must keep in mind that *stress* is an emotional circumstance with physical and emotional manifestations. Therefore, you need to discover and use creative therapies geared toward mental stimulation. Note that emotional stress relief is most effective when the horse is engaged in some form of communicating.

The importance of proper, daily stress dissemination cannot be overlooked as an essential part of any preventive medicine and performance horse training regime. The Thomas Herding Technique uses *Light Touch Therapy* (see p. 32) and formulated stress management protocols that are further developed for the case-specific needs of the individual patient, whether in daily work or convalescing.

Of course, each farm, each training facility, is unique and requires its own environmental assessment. The Thomas Herding Technique can provide a personalized assessment for the horse owner specifically designed to nurture the Natural Herd Dynamic and improve the quality of life of all horses in the domestic environment.

CASE STUDY

The Benefits of Nature Nurturing the Horse: Burchard von Oettingen and the Royal Trakehnen Stud

One of my favorite authors and published sources of the benefits of making the farm environment as natural as possible for the horse is Burchard von Oettingen who, at the turn of the twentieth century, was director of the Royal Trakehnen Stud, where the Trakehner breed evolved, in what was then East Prussia. Von Oettingen was a world-renowned expert on horse care, and in his book, *Horse Breeding in Theory and Practice* (Sampson Low, Marston & Co., 1909), he outlined the benefits of pasturing horses. Although written over 100 years ago, the universality of his writing, extolling the benefits of nature nurturing the horse, bears repeating here:

> *Even the best soil requires, in order to derive any benefit from its advantages for breeding good, capable and sound horses, two very important factors, i.e., paddocks and permanent pastures…But the method of rearing in the stable without paddocks and permanent pastures, which is still so widespread in Germany for all kinds of breeds, threatens to ruin many breedings…Paddocks and permanent pastures serve, therefore, as a contrast to the method of rearing in the stable, to keep the breeding material as long as possible outside the stable and in conformity with nature, to nourish same. The following advantages thus arise:*

1. The influence of light. The recently well recognized beneficial influences of light consist principally in destroying many very dangerous microbes, especially tuberculosis bacilli, and in increasing the energy of life by multiplying the red corpusculli and the haemoglobis.

2. The influence of good air. The air rich in oxygen in the open is a primary condition of every healthy development. The continuous remaining out in the open increases the need of oxygen, and in order to satisfy their needs, horses must, by deep breathing, make a greater use of the lungs. Accordingly, the lungs will be extended and strengthened, and also the energy of life increased.

3. The influence of wind and weather. The constant skin massage by wind and weather strengthens the whole nervous system. As a matter of fact, wind and weather preserves the whole animal organism in a continuous and beneficial training through frequent and sudden changes, and forces it to get accustomed to outside circumstances for the sake of self-preservation. In conjunction with the beneficial influence of light and air, wind and weather, owing to a normal and strengthening development of the nervous system, favour the health in such a good and energetic way altogether impossible if the horses are brought up in the stable.

4. The influence of exercise. A voluntary, continuous and mostly slow exercise on the meadows is necessary when seeking their food. By this means the sinews, muscles and bones are under the influence of a favourable slow, continuous and effective training quite impossible outside of the meadows. The longer grazing is possible…and especially night grazing, the more distinctly is to be observed a favourable development of the formation of the body, especially of the shape of the limbs, as well as that so important to correct walk. The voluntary desire of the horses to visit distinct parts of the meadows, the possibility of their moving about as they please, and so noticing all that is going on around them, the attention which is required for observing changes, the many chances to caper and play with their companions—all these strengthen the intellect and senses, and are the best and only preventives against timidity.

5. Food grazing. The advantages of grazing on the meadow, as against green food in the stable, lie, firstly, in the fact that the horses never get as much in

their mouth in the meadow as in the stable, and that, therefore, sudden over-
loading of the stomach is avoided; secondly, many and just the best and young-
est grasses lose their taste between the time of being mowed and eaten; thirdly,
the useful combination of amids are, for the most part, in the younger plants,
and these are the most difficult to mow, but the horses whilst on the meadow
get them easily. For the good preservation of pastures it is very important that
they should be grazed alternately, as far as possible, by horses, cows or oxen
(but not by sheep).

From the strengthening of bones and tendons as well as the heart, lungs, and limbs by exercise over varying terrain, to the continuous beneficial nurturing provided by environmental stimuli that the casual observer, man, long ago ceased to rely on for survival, indeed, there is no better nurturing process than that provided the horse by Mother Nature. It is not practical to breed or train the equine athlete without fully understanding the "view from the hoof" and the necessity of nature's beneficial nurturing of the horse. Only then can one hope to grasp the reality of the horse and the Equine Circle from the vantage point of man, and do one's best to provide the setting, albeit artificial, where the equine athlete can prosper.

Burchard von Oettingen's work at Trakehnen and other stud farms owned by the Prussian state, such as Beberbeck and Altefeld, was exemplary. During his tenure with the Royal Stud until retirement in 1920, von Oettingen diligently worked to improve the training and stud operation. He rebuilt several of the structures at Trakehnen that had been destroyed by the Russians during World War I, and he designed Altefeld to be a self-sufficient training and breeding facility on a model similar to Trakehnen. Von Oettingen traveled throughout Europe and America to study the operation of other stud farms and racing in those countries.

The Trakehner breed is based on a small East Prussian horse called the "Schwaike," which was known for its phenomenal endurance and versatility. Through the years this local breed was crossed with various larger "imported" stallions to provide mounts for warfare, for general transportation, and for agricultural work. After the establishment of the Royal Stud, select English Thoroughbred and Arabian stallions were purchased and added to the breed. One of von Oettingen's crowning achievements for the improvement of the Royal Stud was the purchase in 1913 of the English-bred Thoroughbred Dark Ronald for £25,000 (about $40,000). It was, definitely, money well spent as Dark Ronald became a foundation stallion of the Royal Stud and one of the most influential sires in the history of Germany.

Dark Ronald
Sire-Line Descendants & German Derby Winners

1920 – Herold	**1944** – Nordlicht[4]	**1993** – Lando[8]
1927 – Mah Jong[1]	**1947** – Singlspieier	**1997** – Borgia[8]
1928 – Lupus[2]	**1948** – Birkhahn[5]	**2005** – Nicaron[8]
1930 – Alba[3]	**1952** – Mangon	
1931 – Dionys[2]	**1960** – Alarich[6]	1 - Sired by Prunus (3)
1932 – Palastpage[1]	**1961** – Baalim[6]	2 - Sired by Herold (3)
1933 – Alchimist[2]	**1976** – Stuyvesant	3 - Sired by Wallenstein (2)
1935 – Sturmvogel[4]	**1977** – Surumu	4 - Sired by Oleander (2)
1938 – Orgelton[1]	**1985** – Acatenango[7]	5 - Sired by Alchimist (2)
1939 – Wehr Dich[3]	**1989** – Mondrian[7]	6 - Sired by Mangon (2)
1940 – Swarzgold[5]	**1991** – Temporal[7]	7 - Sired by Sumuru (3)
		8 - Sired by Acatenango (3)

4.6 Moorlands-Totilas, triple gold medalist at the 2010 World Equestrian Games, is a direct sire-line descendent of Dark Ronald, one of the most influential sires in the history of Germany. Here he is with Edward Gal at the World Equestrian Games in Lexington, Kentucky.

Dark Ronald sired the German Derby winner Herold, and *his* sire line produced other notable Thoroughbreds such as Alchimist, Birkhahn, Surumu, and Acatenango, all of whom were classic champions and important sires. In all, the sire line of Dark Ronald has produced 25 German Derby winners, and his influence has even recently been seen in the United States—as Acatenango is the broodmare sire of Animal Kingdom, winner of the 2011 Kentucky Derby and Eclipse Champion Three-Year-Old Male.

In addition to becoming a tremendous influence on the German Thoroughbred, the sire line of Dark Ronald also is a powerful worldwide influence on the European Warmblood. The highly regarded Moorlands-Totilas, viewed by many as one of the greatest horses in the history of dressage and a triple gold medalist at the 2010 World Equestrian Games in Lexington, Kentucky, is a direct sire-line descendent of Dark Ronald (fig. 4.6). In the show jumping world, Dark Ronald is a direct sire-line ancestor of the deceased jumping champion and influential improvement sire Cor de la Bryére and his sons Caletto I, Caletto II, Caletto III, Calypso I, Calypso II, Calypso III, Calypso IV, Corrado I, Corde-Star, and Cordalmé Z.

The result of von Oettingen's study and labor was the establishment of a first-class breeding and training operation that relied on the foundation principle of making the farm environment as natural as possible in order to produce the healthiest, soundest horses. His efforts were integral to the development of the Trakehner as a performance horse, as it went on in the 1920s and 1930s to win countless medals and awards in jumping, eventing, dressage, and steeplechase.

CASE STUDY

Federico Tesio and the Natural Herd Dynamic

Perhaps, the greatest stud master who understood the Natural Herd Dynamic and agreed with von Oettingen about the importance of making farm life as natural as possible in order to produce happy, healthy, and sound horses was Federico Tesio. Australian bloodstock agent and author Ken McLean, in his book *Tesio: Master of Matings* (Horwitz Grahame, 1984), wrote that Tesio viewed von Oettingen's *Breeding in Theory and Practice* as a "marvelous stimulant," noting that Tesio "gleaned many inspirational ideas" from its pages.

And when one reads translator Edward Spinola's introduction to Tesio's book *Breeding the Racehorse* (JA Allen, 1958), it seems quite obvious that Tesio agreed with von Oettingen about the necessity of an "as natural as possible" existence. According to Spinola, Tesio's Thoroughbred farm Dormello, which was located on the banks of Lake Miaggiore in Northern Italy, had the appearance of an Italian Villa, and it was actually divided into several mini farms complete with their own paddocks and pastures, layered at different elevations among the hills overlooking the lake. In 1933, pedigree authority Friedrich Becker visited several stud farms in Italy, including Tesio's, and in his book, *The Breed of the Racehorse* (British Bloodstock Agency, 1936), Becker elaborated on Tesio's method of raising bloodstock:

> [*Tesio*] *ascribes the successes of his mares mainly to the change of climate and environment to which he is exposing them as many times as it is possible during their stud career…His stud is situated at the banks of the Lago Maggiore, one of the picturesque lakes at the foot of the Alps, and consists of three parts, the first at level with the lake, the second some hundred yards above that level, and the third still higher up in the mountains. According to the time of the year the mares, upon their return from other studs and abroad, are transferred from one part to the other and provisions made for a cold winter when they would be sent south to Mr. Tesio's second stud near Rome. No mare is kept longer than a few months on the same paddock and thus absorbs fresh impressions during the whole time of pregnancy…*
>
> *"I am taking a philosophical aspect of matters," Mr. Tesio observed. "Supposing mankind would be wiped off from the earth by a terrestrial upheaval and horses stay back, do you think mine would remain in the north during the cold season? Certainly not! They would migrate to milder zones and when the weather there becomes too hot, wander northward again. Anyhow, they would keep on changing quarters the whole year round as their prototypes have done. I have come to appreciate the blessings of such changes from the earliest days of my activity as a breeder of racehorses and mainly ascribe my success to the principles of keeping my mares on the move. That's the natural way."*

Indeed, Tesio went to great lengths to make Dormello as natural as possible for his horses. Tesio's practice of sending his weanlings to southern Italy in autumn where they could enjoy an extended grazing season in the warmer climate and boarding during winter at the farm of his racing partner Mario Incisa della

Rochetta produced two of his greatest champion Thoroughbreds: Donatello and Nearco. During his lifetime, Tesio bred and trained at Dormello an incredible 21 Derby Italiano winners.

Nurturing the Natural Herd Dynamic in the domestic environment is essential in providing for the health and well-being of your performance horses and a key element in ensuring soundness, longevity, and competitive success. Not only are horses who are given the freedom to move more physically fit, but a more natural domestic environment makes for an emotionally healthier, happier horse. An understanding of the true herding dynamics of the equine helps the horse owner become a better host for an animal that was not born to know fences or stalls. The environment is the foundation from which all else stems, and it is very often the keeper of unseen stress and behavior issues we only observe much later. The horse owner has the responsibility to fully understand the environment the equine was "built for," and he must do his best to recreate it.

5 Emotional Conformation:
The Secret to Breeding, Buying, and Training Equine Champions

*"A horse gallops with his lungs, perseveres with his heart
and wins with his character."* —Federico Tesio

If anyone ever knew how to embrace the magic within the spirit of the horse, it was Federico Tesio—the Italian horseman you met at the end of the last chapter. Tesio's passion for the horse began at an early age—he spent a lifetime researching and studying everything there was to know about the horse, especially the Thoroughbred. As a young man, he traveled to South America where he broke horses with Gauchos on the Argentine Pampas. He was a "gentleman jockey," participating in over 500 steeplechases throughout Europe. As a breeder and trainer, Tesio was known as the "Wizard of Dormello" and year after year, his stud farm produced one classic champion Thoroughbred after another. Tesio knew how to pick the right bloodlines, and his bloodstock program did much to improve the Thoroughbred breed. Of course Tesio had his share of breeding failures, but for the most part, Tesio knew how to put together all the "puzzle pieces" of the Equine Circle.

The Importance of Breeding for Behavior

Of all the renowned breeders and trainers of Thoroughbreds, Tesio was one of the greatest, and he was keenly aware that breeding for behavior in the horse was in tune with Mother Nature's design for survival and success. A close review of Tesio's own writing shows that not only was he a brilliant pedigree analyst, but he also was an astute student of horse behavior. Or, stated another way, Tesio studied what I call the *Emotional Conformation* of the horse—how the horse's psyche is built. He understood the importance of Emotional Conformation and specifically looked for it, spending hour after hour at auctions studying both the physical and Emotional Conformation of the horses he planned to purchase. In *Tesio: Master of Matings,* author Ken McLean wrote: "[Tesio's] first-hand knowledge of the peculiar characteristics of each individual in his stable, and their subsequent progress on the racetrack, enabled Tesio to be in a unique position to judge whether or not his reasoning behind each mating was accurate or otherwise."

Franco Varola, a noted Italian writer and author instrumental in the development of *Dosage*—a technique for classifying Thoroughbred pedigrees by type—knew Tesio, and he wrote in his book *The Tesio Myth* (JA Allen, 1984) that Tesio often spent hour after hour studying the behavior and reactions of his horses as they moved about in the Dormello stableyard. "The advantage of Tesio as a trainer over everyone else in his profession was precisely that he could afford to study his own horses," noted Varola. "This intensive study could lead him to change distance, or to change riding plates, or to change riding tactics."

In his own right, Varola knew the importance of horse behavior, too. His Dosage system (not the one commonly used today) consisted of five "aptitudinal" groups, and Varola was most interested in the behavioral traits and characteristics that each sire transmitted to his offspring.

"The differences between the five aptitudinal groups are of essence or character," noted Varola in his book *Typology of the Racehorse* (JA Allen, 1974). "It matters very little whether a racehorse is 16 hands or 16.2, or whether it is chestnut or brown; but it does matter a lot the way he behaves in actual racing, whether he is consistent or erratic, brilliant or slow, bellicose or resigned, in other words which pattern or mode of being is he expressing…It is of great utility to be able to distinguish between these various aptitudes, this being something that plays an effective part in mating."

Nature's Design

Physical genetics breeds the horse; behavioral genetics produces the athlete. Designed by man, the Thoroughbred, the Dutch Warmblood, the Quarter Horse are all hybrid animals. The abrasive nature of man selectively breeding for speed, stamina, beauty, and strength, and nature's quest to breed for survival are antagonistic one to another. As a breeder, we can try to breed the perfect horse from a physical conformation standpoint, but if we ignore the forces of natural selection at work in our breeding stock, we will produce an inferior animal.

Nature's successful breeding program allows a basic physical standard to be necessarily controlled by variations of behavior or *personalities*. Every family member has to be able to fill a role to make the equine herd a success, and it is the diversity of behavior that allows the herd sustainability over time and in changing environmental circumstances.

Physical evolution is the body's adjustment to new and changing environments, which occur as a result of a mental recognition that change is needed in order to survive. In other words, if the horse recognized that he had to climb higher and higher elevations to reach good food and water, over time, the equine body would adapt to the requirements necessary to reach it. What this means to a breeding program, and indeed to training protocol, is that behavior is the most important trait to look for.

Siblings Aren't the Same

Any breeder will tell you that you can breed a high standing sire to a wonderful, proven mare, and two of their full-blood offspring, seemingly equal in physical stature and racing, dressage, or reining ability, will often display vast differences in performance levels on the racetrack or in the show ring. One horse may be an excellent runner while the other is a mediocre or poor runner. One horse may have a spectacular piaffe while the other is nothing special. At stud, the excellent performer may produce offspring that are less talented while the mediocre horse produces offspring that excel in competition. Both horses have the same genetic origin, and yet, their performance history and the performance history of their offspring can be vastly different (figs. 5.1 A & B).

Indeed, *physical* genetics alone is not the determining factor for athletic success or failure. It is the mind of the horse that is in complete control of his "will" and "drive," and thus, his performance, on and off the racetrack, in and out of the show ring. While physical ability is important, *the mental capacity of the equine controls the physical output of the athlete.*

Revisiting the Puzzle

In order to understand and identify the various traits and characteristics that make up the horse, we must first recognize the intent of nature's stud master. As we've already discussed, Mother Nature has designed the horse to live in a group, the

5.1 A & B Barbaro (#5), winner of the 2006 Kentucky Derby, is an example of the highest level of Herd Dynamic (A). Not only could he identify and manage stimulus while in motion, Barbaro was adept at targeting and releasing opponents. Shown here winning the Holy Bull Stakes early in his three-year-old season, Barbaro's right ear is feeling the horse behind him while his left ear is feeling ahead for additional challenges. Barbaro is an example of what can happen when an excellent physical athlete also has a superior mind.

Barbaro's full sibling Lentenor also was able to interpret multiple stimuli while in motion (B). Lentenor (#2) has a look of calm control despite being in heavy traffic in this photo. Although Lentenor had some of the tenacity we saw in his brother, he lacked Barbaro's ability to efficiently target and release, which led to him "buddying up" during some of his races (see p. 113).

Equine Circle, and has masterfully crafted each horse to fit into the circle like the pieces of a puzzle.

Try as we might to manipulate the puzzle, we can never artificially manufacture what nature provides—all we can do is tinker with what already exists. We know that nature's intent for the horse is to have sustainable survival within a group, or Herd Dynamic.

So how do we put the puzzle together?

Nature adjusts itself over time to fit properly into changing environments, and once accomplished—the physical living conditions having dictated physical properties—we essentially have a standardized end result or *breed types,* which are in essence the characteristics of that physical standard. The physical breed has some variation owing to the mixture of physical genetics that lean toward certain traits over others, but it never strays too far outside the basic platform or it would be a different physical breed altogether.

Nature, however, also allows for certain complexities within any Herd Dynamic. A sustainable herd can only be such when a group with similar physical features and abilities is layered with variable behavioral types. Structure in a group is nature's weapon against time and attrition, and this *order,* overlaid with individual behavioral dynamics, is what allows the pieces of the puzzle to fit together for group survival.

Pedigrees, bloodlines, and physical conformation layered over with individual Emotional Conformation, should be the primary consideration when selecting horses for a breeding program or competition barn. You can train the mind of the horse to get the most from his body. So, then, you should breed and buy for mental aptitude that will allow the horse to live up to his fullest potential.

Introduction to Emotional Conformation Profiling

Whether buying, selling, training, or breeding, *all* horses are graded on their *conformation,* which is an analysis of the overall *physical* horse and how he's put together. This is standard procedure throughout the horse industry and across disciplines. In addition to *physical conformation,* I grade a horse's *Emotional Conformation.* This is the term I use to describe the psychology of the horse, and I use it to analyze the behavioral dynamics, as well as the social tendencies, that impact the potential of the individual horse.

Because the overall mental capacity and aptitude of each horse is made up of both seen and unseen *Emergent Properties* and *tendencies of behavior* (see p. 1), the mental preparedness of a horse to react and interact with environmental and social dynamics becomes a vital indicator of his performance ability and a source of important information (fig. 5.2). It matters not whether I am preparing an *Emotional Conformation Profile*—a kind of personality test—of an equine-assisted therapy horse, a high-end racing Thoroughbred, or a competitive dressage horse, Emotional Conformation is *the indicator* of that horse's athletic ability. Understanding this is important if the owner or trainer is going to help that horse become a successful competitor.

Reviewing the Horse's Layers of Growth and Learning

Early in this book we discussed how mentally, the horse is nurtured and grows in layers of experiences (memories), with acquired instinct gradually "overlaying" the basic instinct inherent at birth. The acquired instinct is *learned* instinct—as the horse expands his experiences and begins to differentiate between stimuli, associative triggers are recorded and the act of learning, good or bad, takes place.

5.2 How a horse reacts to new stimulus in a sale environment can tell you a lot about how efficient an athlete the horse can be. This weanling has close space issues. I am posing no threat, yet the horse remains flighty and overly cautious for too long.

All horses are very similar in the initial "ingredients" of their Emotional Conformation—the basic instinct is layered with acquired instinct along with the ability to assimilate in environments in order to survive. The fork in the road is within the developing and very individualized *Personality Propensity*—the horse's ability to focus, manage, and interpret—and the resulting "spin" the individual takes on acquired instincts and associative triggers. Emotional Conformation Profiling is the study of both the horse's acquired instincts and his Personality Propensities.

The Pilot of the Machine

If we believe that each horse has obvious individual *personality traits* in addition to *physical characteristics,* then we must also realize that the horse is more dependent on one of these than the other for survival. In a manner of speaking, the

5.3 A & B A big part of the Emotional Conformation inspection process is observation and study. Here I am at the 2011 Keeneland November Breeding Stock Sale, watching a weanling walk up the chute into the main sale pavilion (A). When constructing an Emotional Conformation Profile, it's important to see how long it takes a horse to process new information, how much body language he exerts, how he moves into space, and how he manages stimuli. I begin my investigation of a different horse from a relative distance (B).

machine of the horse is his *physical conformation.* The *pilot* of that machine is his *Emotional Conformation.*

When profiling for Emotional Conformation, I observe the horse to identify unique pieces of his Individual Horse Personality (see p. 17). The individual nuances, behavioral tendencies, Emergent Properties, and obvious behavioral dynamics, are all the parts of the equine psyche or *mental aptitude* (figs. 5.3 A & B). When fit together, a very unique *profile* comes into view.

I offer Emotional Conformation Profiling in two formats. There is a *basic profile,* which is an initial developmental effort, and there is a more detailed and protracted full-on *investigation* that results in a report where you can expect, depending on your area of need, an investigative summary, training protocol/recommendations, and analysis. We'll examine the profiling process in detail in the next chapter (see p. 77).

Physical Conformation Offers an Incomplete Picture

Physical conformation only gives you a partial glance at the ability of an individual horse. If we take the Thoroughbred, for example, history is replete with racehorses who had less-than-perfect conformation but went on to win classic and handicap stakes races. (Note: all amounts listed in British pounds are approximate.)

- **Lookin At Lucky** was a buy-back for $35,000 (£23,000) at the 2008 Keeneland September Yearling Sale (fig. 5.4). From the knees up, Lookin At Lucky was a beautiful horse. But below the knees, the beauty ended. He had narrow feet, lesions in his stifles and front ankles, and his pasterns were too long. However, despite those conformation flaws, Lookin At Lucky had the will to win and he became a classic champion Thoroughbred when he won the Preakness Stakes in 2010. In addition, Looking At Lucky won four grade one stakes and three grade two stakes races en route to earning an Eclipse Champion Male Award as a two- and three-year-old, and becoming the only horse to achieve that honor since Spectacular Bid. Not too shabby for less-than-perfect physical specimen.

5.4 Lookin At Lucky, winner of the 2010 Preakness Stakes, failed to sell as a yearling, but the May foal began to bloom when given a chance to show his patterns of motion at the 2009 Keeneland April sale of selected two-year-olds in training. Despite less-than-perfect physical conformation, Lookin At Lucky was a classic champion of his generation thanks to his strong Emotional Conformation.

- **Real Quiet** only fetched $17,000 (£11,000) at the 1996 Keeneland September Yearling Sale, compared to the average of $46,978 (around £30,000). His frame was so narrow that Thoroughbred trainer Bob Baffert nicknamed him "The Fish." Turf writer Jay Privman made this observation of Real Quiet in a 1998 *New York Times* article: "In a sport where yearling horses often cost more than a four-bedroom house, Real Quiet was a fixer-upper in a rundown neighborhood. He had a crooked right front leg, a moderate pedigree, and was sold at auction in a cattle call that finds nearly 3,000 horses going through the sales ring in a week." Despite his flaws, Real Quiet won the 1998 Kentucky Derby and the Preakness, and barely missed sweeping the Triple Crown with a loss by a nose to Victory Gallop in the Belmont Stakes (fig. 5.5).

- **Sunday Silence,** according to Turf writer William Knack in a 1989 *Sports Illustrated article,* "was a badly cow-hocked youngster—seen from directly behind, his rear legs were, in effect, knock-kneed and toed-out, like a cow's, rather than straight, as is normal in a horse. He looked like a colt who would never make it to the races." Sunday Silence failed to sell as a yearling and as a two-year-old because of his physical flaws, but those defects did not affect his performance on the racetrack. His epic battles with Easy Goer in the Triple Crown races—in which Sunday Silence won the Kentucky Derby and Preakness Stakes—are a testament to his never-ceasing spirit and fervent will to win. Turf writer Jay Hovdey in a 2002 *Daily Racing Form* article eulogizing the death of Sunday Silence at the age of 16 said it best: "There was nothing pretty about him, save for a coat dark as a gunfighter's heart. Hocks knocking and back at the knees, Sunday Silence made fools of the conformation gurus who said he would never last. Those same fools were afraid he would spread those flaws at stud, and so they let him go. The joke was

5.5 1998 Kentucky Derby winner Real Quiet is yet another example of how the mental capacity of the equine controls the physical output of the athlete. Real Quiet was crooked and thin-framed, but when traveling in a herd at a classic distance, he proved to be a champion.

on them, exquisite in its execution, eternal in its consequences. Sunday Silence turned into an expatriate hero, shunned by the country of his birth, adopted by a racing culture on the rise. Thriving at stud in Japan, the Kentucky reject became the most valuable animal in the world, generating as much as $50 million in fees each year. His name was gold, his image revered. Even the glyph of his blaze—a writhing white mushroom cloud—could be found adorning souvenirs throughout the faraway land."

- **Seattle Slew** was originally rejected by Keeneland sales officials from being listed in the 1975 Summer Yearling Sale because of his pedigree and appearance. Seattle Slew toed-out in his right front foot, which is viewed by some horsemen as a serious conformation flaw, and which is most likely why he only fetched the price of $17,500 (£11,000) at the Fasig-Tipton Lexington Yearling Sale. However, despite his flaw, Seattle Slew went on to make racing history by becoming the tenth Triple Crown winner and the only horse to accomplish that feat with a perfect undefeated racing record.

Kerry's Corner

Question: **Can you elaborate a little more on your thoughts in the area of Emotional Conformation as it pertains to training and breeding horses and herd social structures? I have little doubt that your efforts here will have influence on a larger spectrum of animal species and how we as fellow researchers and trainers and breeders consider the tasks before us.** —University Professor/Researcher

Answer: It is my opinion that *mental evolution* paves the way for the physical changes and that social/herd species use *nurturing* to advance survival. The physical survival of a species of animal living in a herd or a group, such as horses or even primates, I feel, is highly dependent on the psychological relationships between the members. Each individual is dependent on himself and the other group members for daily life, requiring a necessary interaction on an Emotional Conformation level. To be sustained, this platform is influenced by what can be called "decisions" based on interactions with others and the environment, and more importantly, on interpretation of the environmental stimuli. Herd animals move toward food and water sources when they are thirsty or hungry, or seek minerals as needed. Decision based on need is nonetheless decision just the same, and thus a physical response. If your food source is at high elevation, the body evolves to fit the decision made over time. Evolution mandates that physical change is made in order to survive or sustain group survival.

Using the concept of "ingredients," I seek to understand a species of social-seeking animals (like horses) by studying the way an individual fits within the group.

- **Northern Dancer** did not meet the reserve price of $25,000 (£16,000) at the yearling sales because of his small "runty" size. Northern Dancer eventually stood just over 15 hands, which was still small in comparison to other Thoroughbreds. But, what he lacked in stature, he made up with heart and his will to win. Northern Dancer won the 1964 Kentucky Derby (setting a new track record) and the Preakness Stakes, and at stud, he became one of the greatest sires of the twentieth century.

- **Seabiscuit** was an "ugly duckling" as a foal, and his looks did not improve with age. He was a knobby-kneed, short, blunt, ragged racehorse who displayed a wild thrashing and flailing of his left foreleg as he raced around the track. But in the hands of trainer Tom Smith, Seabiscuit became the Champion Handicap Division Horse in 1937 and 1938, and he was the 1938 Horse of the Year. By the time of his retirement, Seabiscuit had become the all-time leading money earner with $437,730 (£280,000) in career earnings. (See more of his story beginning on p. 157.)

Emotional Conformation is the foundation of *individualism,* which allows both physical and behavioral genetics to be handed down the line as nature fills out her ranks according to need. This is not to be confused with *according to our need.* In fact, a serious oversight in breeding programs is that we breed horses, or any animal for that matter, to physically fit a mold we're artificially designing, and we ask Mother Nature to follow *our* guideline. We certainly can manipulate fairly well at least the *physical* genetic result. However, there is a problem inherent in this approach, which is that far too often we do not consider, or apply to the equation, the *behavioral* genetics of the two horses we match. If we allow that animals like horses have a *personality,* should we not then allow for this truth to be a vital part of herd structuring, breeding, and training?

When you know your horse, you can *communicate your intent.* Goal achievement and partnership with the horse rests deep within your ability to communicate your intent…and training is communication. You may know your horse as he reflects your desires, but how well do you know your horse when he is not reacting to *your* needs and requirements?

Emotional Conformation Profiling seeks to identify the ingredients that make up your horse. Once this information is attained, you can compare this to your goal, or your *intentions* for the ingredients. If you find that you're not pushing a round peg into a square hole, the process— be it training or breeding—then comes down to your communication of intent, as well as consideration of both *physical genetic ability* and *behavioral genetic capacity.*

5.6 The more sale horses I inspect, the more I realize that some commercial Thoroughbred breeders are focusing too much on physical conformation and not enough on mental soundness. This young horse—a broodmare prospect—is internalizing her fear, which will delay the interpretation of stimuli. This frozen-in-time expression indicates to me that the time it takes for her to interpret the cause of influence might be too protracted, and she may well default to relying on others for direction and security—not an acquired instinct I look for in a trainable athletic mind.

Of course, physical conformation is always an important factor to consider when purchasing a horse for a competitive career. But, as you can see from the list of horses on the pages prior, conformation was *not* a factor in their success on the track—or at stud in the case of Sunday Silence, Seattle Slew, and Northern Dancer. (Real Quiet and Seabiscuit were moderate performers in the breeding shed. Lookin At Lucky stood his first year at stud in 2011.) If you had relied on physical conformation alone when deciding whether or not to purchase those horses, you would have likely missed out on the opportunity to own a champion (fig. 5.6). Emotional Conformation can reveal if the horse has the heart and mind of a potential champion, and it can often trump physical conformation and pedigree. The Emotional Conformation of the previously mentioned Thoroughbreds propelled them to greatness. Their *mental aptitude,* combined with their *physical talent,* set them apart and made them a success.

Why Emotional Conformation Is Important in Sport Horse Breeding

Emotional genetics are revealed in the Emotional Conformation of the horse. Nature has taught us that through natural selection it will always "win in the end" by destroying the antagonistic traits within the species, starting over again, or simply allowing another species to fill the gap. The modern day sport horse is comprised of individually handed down parts from two or even three "base species" blended together. Because we breed two physically different performers doesn't mean that we have shuffled the genetic deck of cards enough to produce a champion equine athlete.

Consider the breeding line of the horse as a gene pool much like a baseball team with a roster of fifteen individual players. Out of the fifteen players, only nine can be on the field at any given time. These nine players are the representatives for the entire team. We can take that team to the World Series and shuffle the roster, changing player lineup and field position, but we are still playing with the same basic team, no matter how much shuffling we make. Breeding the sport horse by looking only at the pedigrees of the mates is simply shuffling the team members around. It's a crap shoot, a roll of the dice. Still, we breed and breed and try to force the issue, even if it takes 100 times or more to produce that one homerun, that one winner.

If behavior is not considered in the selection of breeding stock, at best we are rolling the dice in our breeding program. Helter-skelter breeding, also, is rolling the dice. Breeding one year to this, the second year to something different, so on and so forth, allows for a constant state of confusion, and it will do much damage to sport horse breeds. When we select breeding stock only based on pedigree, physical conformation, and money earned or medals won, we are overlooking the process of natural selection. If we do this often enough, there will be a weakening of the breed in question.

For example, it could be argued—and it is by some—that more than any other breed, the Thoroughbred as a *sound* animal is on the decline. This, if it is true, is our fault. We cannot continually remove the element of natural selection from the process and expect great results without weakening the breed. This is antagonistic to the evolutionary process of assimilation.

We are not breeding deer, though we expect the sport horse to run and jump like one—fast as the wind, over long periods of time and variable terrain, with an ever-weakening physical constitution and erratic ability to focus. Because we mate two incredibly talented athletes with outstanding pedigrees doesn't mean that their progeny will also be outstanding. Instead the result is overbreeding and a saturation of the industry with far too many mediocre horses deemed unworthy of financial support because *they don't win,* or are *unsound* and *breakdown.* Indeed, we find time and again that breeding sport horses is not an assembly line activity and should not be approached like one. Nature has a rule for the hybrid species that no human can replace by simply "shuffling the genetic deck of cards." Nature's law includes the rules of *atavism*—the tendency to revert to ancestral type. A hybrid of *any species,* much like the Thoroughbred, the Warmblood, and the Quarter Horse, will seek to return to its most naturally occurring form because it seeks out *optimum survivability.*

Breeding Synergy in an Artificial Herd

A tremendous amount of research and consideration is in play when it comes to breeding the sport horse. Conformation, achievements, and history are all key components breeders use when hedging their bets that their young stock will measure up to their intent. But how often does that really happen?

When considering which horses to mate, the very first question that must be answered is, "How well will the mind run the body I make from that mating?" Therefore, the governing factor of any performance horse breeding program should be the Emotional Conformation Profiles of the horses on the season's short list. Without considering Emotional Conformation in your breeding plan, you at best have a 1 in 4 and, at worst, a 1 in 8 chance of getting the behavioral genetics necessary to get the best performance from your equine athlete. This is why so many *good-looking horses* just don't seem to have the necessary *giddy-up* to go. Breeding in large numbers is not the answer. Sure, your chances of getting the formula just right by *chance* increases with more matings, but this manner of breeding only creates a large number of horses that will never make it to the show pen or racetrack.

Consider again what Mother Nature designed the horse for: herd living. The herd is generally made up of three to six horses in a family unit. Often in a herd you will find that nature provides the proper pieces in the proper proportions to sustain itself, with the mares of the herd being the only real constant.

A stallion leader may only be with the herd for one to three mating seasons before a new stallion overtakes him to ensure herd diversity. If able, during his time with the herd, the stallion will most likely breed the same mares at least two consecutive seasons. During this time he produces, even from the same mare, different behavioral genetics with very similar physical traits (as we discussed earlier—see p. 57). This is nature's design. Then the herd will have a *physical standard that is consistent with a varying but closely related behavioral aspect.* This creates a "unit," and we can use this same approach in our breeding program to create an *artificial herd* If you have a proper breeding match, both physically and behaviorally, your chances of getting your *intended* product increases dramatically—provided you maintain consistency and breed the same sire to two or three mares with similar physical makeup but complementary mental differences for a minimum of two, if not three, years in a row. In doing so, you are managing your herd in a way that more closely mirrors nature's original plan by reapplying an element of natural selection in the breeding of your bloodstock.

What Makes the Difference?

To build a *foundation herd,* breeding for mental consistency far outweighs breeding for physical conformation. As I've mentioned already in this book, nature has provided us with a standard mantra that should not be forgotten: *The mental capacity of the equine controls the physical output of the athlete* (figs. 5.7 A–C).

Nature provides the horse with the mental capacity he needs, exactly fitted to the requirements necessary to survive in his environment. Think of the differences in horse size and mentality from breed to breed. A look back in history reveals that the successful species was always matched naturally, mind to body. Indeed, for a species on the evolutionary move forward, mental capacity is *greater* than physical ability: mental agility and focus are well suited to enable survival within a given

5.7 A–C Here, I am profiling a Hat Trick filly at the 2011 Fasig-Tipton Kentucky October Yearling Sale at Newtown Paddocks in Lexington, Kentucky. The filly shows excellent distance focus, locking onto me as she approaches (A).

5.7 A–C *continued* The filly moves into space well and does not shy from my space infraction (B). One of the key behavioral genetics I have seen in the Thoroughbred sire Hat Trick and his offspring is the ability to focus, identify, and interpret stimulus at great distances in front of them.

This Hat Trick colt at the same sale also shows strong forward focus ability (C). In a training and racing capacity, that means these two horses can move confidently into space instead of backing out of space. It is a very positive behavioral trait for a racehorse to have, and one that should be bred for.

environment. This aspect of natural selection allows for growth and development in the horse, and it is what we should breed for in our equine athletes.

The Need for Natural Selection

The artificial environment does not allow for the natural selection process to take place as we quite often select and arrange matings by pedigree. This doesn't mean an element of natural selection cannot be "inserted" into the artificial human environment. Allowance for what is innate within the horse is a major factor in adding this element, and it economizes owner and breeder investment while advancing the overall welfare of horses—with this in mind, it should top our list of industry priorities. Emotional Conformation Profiling of horses intended to be bred can provide the extra information needed to increase the probability of a more successful outcome.

Some *personality types* just shouldn't be mated—it is a bad investment. The survival of a species designed to live in a social environment, where each is dependent on the other for survival, does not mate blindly. In the wild it is actually something of an anomaly when the lead stallion and mare breed and produce a natural lead horse who will one day take over the herd or another band of horses. In truth, it is often a lead stallion mated with an adjutant mare that produces a horse physically and mentally capable of leading the herd.

Conversely, it is also just as likely for a subordinate stallion to mate with the lead or adjutant mare. The reason for this is hidden within the evolution of survival: sustainability in life requires a constant influx of motion, even within a social group. In fact, all of the previous scenarios are fairly equal in their likelihood of breeding a *herd leader*. This is because it is the Emotional Conformation of the individual horse that determines leadership. When viewing horses in the wild, it is normal for the old and nearly decrepit mare to lead the herd to water, food, and down through the mountains to safer places—that the leader has survived to old age is evidence of natural selection and evolution.

When breeding for competitive success, it is important to remember how the process of evolution actually occurs. We look at old pictures of horses, and we are fascinated by the physical changes that have occurred in various breeds over time. We have bred our show horses and racehorses based on how their physical makeup will operate in a given environment. For example, a Thoroughbred may be bred to perform on a certain surface—dirt, turf, or synthetic. But how the horse's body is made to move over a given surface is not nearly as important as how the horse's mental capacity is equipped to interpret the environmental stimulus. *Physical evolution is secondary to mental evolution.* Decision-making ability *stimulates* physical change, not the other way around. The horse has an incredible ability to assimilate mentally. This is why understanding the individual horse's Emotional Conformation plays an integral part in producing the successful equine athlete. It is the key to breeding success.

Breeding Forward

Breeding for behavior requires an established Emotional Conformation Profile for either the proposed sire or the proposed broodmare, after which a mate can be sought to suit the stallion or mare and the desired projection or *likely foal tendencies.* The highest probability of success requires considering and combining both

Kerry's Corner

Question: **A good friend of mine and I have been considering options in regards to a "reshuffling" of her stable, and I thought I would ask where the *real* emphasis should be in one's breeding program? My friend is not a "big name breeder" and needs to optimize her funds to stay in the game. Does she focus on developing the "herd" with one new stallion for breeding, or keep a few sires and find a few good "girls"? There are lots of "formulas" for this I think—do you have one?** —Maria, Argentina

Answer: I really love this question because it addresses something very important, which I call the *Economics of Behavior.* "Optimizing resources" is a good way to put it, and "staying in the [breeding] game," so to speak, demands more information in order to make better decisions.

My "formula" is more of an equation: successful breeding is taking the *Now Properties* of proposed sire (that which is self-evident in the stallion during his life, and not so much his ancestral propensities) and matching them with *Emergent Properties* of the proposed broodmare (those things that are being advanced into the foal that are latent at times in the broodmare).

Competitive survival mandates female superiority over foal tendencies. In other words, if you like formulas: *Now Properties* (m) + *Emergent Properties* (f) = proportional advancement of competitive "survivalism" in the result (foal).

It is a battle of attrition that breeds mediocrity and even weakens a species by selectively mating horses by way of role-reversal. The horse did not evolve on the course of evolution because of a scattering of individuals and indiscriminate mating strewn across a beach like sea turtles hatching out; rather the horse survives because of careful selection in a contained social unit. Indiscriminate breeding would have been mass suicide.

In an artificial breeding environment it is most important to do all that is feasible to apply, or rather, to *allow* some natural selection into the picture. To achieve this artificially, one should have a good comprehension of the *Emergent Properties* within the broodmares in one's herd.

the *physical* and *emotional genetics* of the individual horses. Evaluations can be most efficacious when working off the short list provided by the owner or pedigree consultant for both mating prospects, as well as pre-purchase evaluations. The Emotional Conformation Profile allows the horse owner to make smarter business decisions and increases the probability of better breeding success. As mentioned, breeding for behavior plays a huge part in increasing the probability of success in the show ring or on the racetrack by decreasing the overbreeding problem of mating 20 horses in hope of producing one or two champions.

Foundation breeding is another avenue to reinvent a way for natural selection to provide for a more stable herd in an artificial environment. Foundation breeding—establishing a strong line clearly demonstrating a *foundation sire* or *mare's* traits and characteristics—happens quite naturally in wild horse herds and is top on the list of an ongoing evolutionary process. It must be noted that we cannot make a mistake of thinking that the evolutionary process is not at work in the domestic horse—it is alive and well, and its job is to advance the species forward, giving it the mental ability to assimilate the body to ever-changing stimuli. This is an important factor that must be considered when developing training protocols and mating selections.

Foundation breeding is *sustainable capacity mating:* your output (foals) will be more likely to meet that which you intend (competitive equine athletes) on a more consistent basis. You can work toward building a foundation with one stallion and one or two broodmares. Once you have found the desired physical conformation you want, you must then mate two horses with the likeliest Emotional Conformation in order to advance the behavioral traits most likely to produce a champion equine athlete.

Sustainable capacity mating is *breeding forward.* Consistency in your breeding program must also allow for the infusion of an outsider. The introduction of a new stallion to a key mare or two enables *forward motion* (in an evolutionary sense) in your herd. To ensure the survival of the species, Mother Nature has established the Herd Dynamic in such a way that foundation mares in a wild herd will, at times, be mated with rogue stallions outside the herd. The importance of this in the artificial environment and selected mating should be a cornerstone. If you have five closely related mares in your foundation herd, do not breed all five to only one sire in your effort to sustain the foundation. Your foundation line is *not* governed by the influence of the stallion, but by your mares. Saturating your group with only one sire will diminish the power of the line, and it will eventually die out. The outcome of such breeding practices will result in horses that are poor competitors and vulnerable to breaking down.

The Winning Formula

When asked for my thoughts about breeding theories and formulas and how natural selection impacts the outcome of a selected mating, a *formula* I use is the following: successful breeding is taking the *Now Properties* of a proposed sire and matching them with the *Emergent Properties* of a proposed broodmare. *Now Properties* are those propensities that are self-evident in the stallion during his life and do not refer so much to his ancestral propensities. *Emergent Properties* of the female are those influences, sometimes latent in the broodmare, that are advanced into the foal. This is nature's key to sustaining a species that is forced to continue to manifest itself by virtue of assimilation to both herd social structures and environmental demands. In the wild, *Competitive survival mandates female superiority over foal tendencies.* In other words, the *Now Properties* of the sire plus the *Emergent Properties* of the broodmare equals nature's proportional advancement of competitive survival in the herd, resulting in the birth of a new foal.

I certainly acknowledge that the sire and his pedigree cannot be overlooked, but in my opinion, far too much emphasis is placed upon the sire. The broodmare is just as important and actually has more influence over the foal because the esoteric *Emergent Properties* of the mare's Emotional Conformation allow for advancement of the *Now Properties* of the sire.

Any species that *adapts* well is a species reliant on a continued advancement of Emergent Properties. The question that we've asked ourselves already in this book is: How do you take *what is* to the next level toward *what could be?* What exists can only be advanced when influenced by what is yet to be, represented in the horse by the ongoing development of *Emergent Properties,* which are born out of continued assimilation. Evolutionary processes thus become self-sustaining so that life can emerge. Because the broodmare is the foundation of a herd group, *she* is the one responsible for passing on and advancing the properties that allow the stallion to lead and protect *in his lifetime.* He only needs to be great *now,* while the mare has to pass on greatness later in order to maintain the herd. This is done in the form of nurturing the mental capacity (Emotional Conformation) that is necessary for a species dependent on social interaction for its continued growth.

"Seeing" the Horse's Morale

In summation, the genetics of behavior are revealed within the Emotional Conformation of the horse, affecting the horse in all areas. Breeding without this consideration will eventually weaken the breed, and this is self-evident. In contrast, breeding
for behavior will improve the breed and limit overbreeding in a random gamble for
a winner, which so often culminates in suffering on the part of the equine species.

Federico Tesio openly embraced the magic within the spirit of the horse, and
that is why he was one of the greatest Thoroughbred breeders of all time. Tesio
knew the importance of Emotional Conformation in breeding, buying, and training the Thoroughbred. He knew it was integral to producing champion racehorses.
One of the best summations of Tesio's knowledge of Emotional Conformation and
his success as a horseman comes from Mario Incisa della Rochetta who was a close
friend and business partner with Tesio in the Dormello Stud for 20 years. In his
book, *The Tesios—As I Knew Them* (JA Allen, 1979), Rochetta wrote:

> We used to play a game at Dormello. Tesio, Donna Lydia [Tesio's wife], my
> wife and I would each select our choice from the current crop of yearlings. The
> names would be put in a sealed envelope to be opened a couple of years later.
> When this happened, Tesio's intuition was apparent, although it would have
> been impossible to define the basis on which he had made his choice, for it was
> certainly not based on conformation. Eventually I became convinced that Tesio
> had the knack to see into a horse's "morale."

Federico Tesio—
The "Wizard of Dormello"

Indeed, Tesio had the knack to see the "morale" of the horse. The knowledge he gleaned from the writings of Burchard von Oettingen (see p. 48) and his lifelong experience interacting with the horse aptly conditioned him as a keen observer of the horses' Emotional Conformation. During his lifetime, The "Wizard of Dormello" bred and trained numerous champion Thoroughbreds—here are some them.

Tesio's Two-Year-Old Champions

Gran Criterium

(1500 Meters)

1913 – Fausta
1916 – Gianpietrina
1919 – Ghiberti
1921 – Melozzo da Forli'
1922 – Cima da
      Conegliano
1929 – Gerard
1931 – Iacopa del Sellaio
1932 – Dossa Dossi
1936 – Donatello II
1937 – Nearco
1940 – Niccolo' dell'Arca
1941 – Donatella
1947 – Trevisana
1948 – Mignard
1950 – Daumier
1954 – Ribot

Criterium Nazionale

(1200 Meters)

1909 – Giottina
1919 – Ghiberti
1920 – Michelangelo
1921 – Nomellina
1922 – Cima da
      Conegliano
1923 – Turletta
1929 – Gerard
1930 – Nogara
1935 – Marieschi
1936 – Donatello II
1937 – Nearco
1945 – Romanella
1947 – Trevisana
1949 – Nattier
1950 – Daumier
1951 – Laszlo

1952 – La Clementina
1953 – Botticelli
1954 – Ribot
1955 – Barbara Sirani
1956 – Grigoresco

Premio Bimbi

(1000 Meters)

1903 – Verrocchia
1904 – Ingegna
1909 – Tanagra
1910 – Guido Reni
1913 – Fausta
1917 – Burne Jones
1918 – Canova
1925 – Apelle
1926 – Galleria Barberini
1930 – Nogara (dh)
1932 – Dossa Dossi
1933 – Bernina
1939 – De Ferrari
1940 – Niccolo'
      dell'Arca
1953 – Giambellina
1956 – Grigoresco

(dh): dead-heat with Camerano

Making the Grade:
How Emotional Conformation Profiling Works

*"It is a trainable mind that will allow the owner, rider, and trainer
to get maximum value out of his or her investment."*

While the journey that began on page one of this book is far from over, like Federico Tesio, you are well on your way to becoming a keen observer of the horse's Emotional Conformation and benefiting from that understanding. You have learned how to enter into the Equine Circle and seen the necessity of nurturing the Natural Herd Dynamic in the artificial, domestic environment in order to create a lifestyle that is beneficial for the physical and emotional well-being of the horse. You have now seen the importance of Emotional Conformation Profiling in breeding, buying, and training horses, and you may have some idea as to how it can give you a clear picture of the emotional health of *all* the horses in your stable, as well as the "star potential" of your equine athletes.

All of these aspects of what I call the *Thomas Herding Technique (THT)* strive to help you be diligent in your efforts to create an environment that promotes the physical and emotional health of your horses. What you've read thus far served as a necessary introduction to what you'll read next—a more complex examination of THT and Emotional Conformation Profiling.

Early Origins of the Thomas Herding Technique

In my early days researching wild Mustangs in the Bighorn Mountains, I had no idea what my study would reveal about the lifestyle and behavior of the Spanish *mesteño*. I was interested in researching the social dynamics of the horse and how those dynamics affected the herd and family unit. Over time, I developed an interest, not in *what* I was looking at (it was obvious these were horses), but in *who* these horses were as *individuals*.

I soon realized that because I am color blind, the usual means of easily identifying horses, sometimes from a distance, by coat color would not work. A new method of identifying the horses had to be implemented. Out of pure necessity, I began to catalog the horses based on individual personality types and the ways in which they communicated (fig. 6.1). Once I began to hone this technique of identifying herd members by their individuality, a larger picture, previously unseen to me, was born.

A Closer Look at the Emotional Conformation Profile

I introduced you to Emotional Conformation and my system of horse profiling in chapter 5 (see p. 55). To recap, an Emotional Conformation Profile can best be described as an attempt to fit together the pieces of the puzzle of an individual horse's behavior. I designed this "personality test," the result of my study and research of

6.1 Sometimes male horses form small bachelor herds and share leadership with one another in order to take advantage of individual strengths. This was one of the many discoveries I made when studying the Emotional Conformation and social dynamics of the wild herds in the Bighorn Mountains.

the wild horse herds, to measure the behavior of the horse. The Emotional Confor-mation Profile was then reworked as necessary so that it was relevant when applied to horses living in a domestic environment. *The environment is the only thing that changes.* The subject matter and the way Emotional Conformation is determined is mostly the same.

Today, the Emotional Conformation Profile is used to measure the mental capacity, aptitude, and mental soundness of the equine athlete to see if he is capable of capitalizing on his physical potential. One of the key things I look for in a horse is a "trainable mind," for it is this that will allow the owner, rider, and trainer to get maximum value out of his or her investment.

The Emotional Conformation Profile I use is made up of 28 different, though congruent, "answers" to behavioral and personality "questions." Since, obviously, the horse is incapable of writing answers to my questions on a piece of paper, I have to *observe* and *investigate* the horse in as noninvasive a manner as possible, in as many different but normally occurring circumstances as there are in a given environment (figs. 6.2 A–K).

Earlier in this book we likened the Equine Circle to a jigsaw puzzle. In keep-ing with this simile, we can say that preparing an Emotional Conformation Profile is also like putting together a puzzle. Imagine a 1,000-piece jigsaw puzzle inside a box. On the cover of the box is the picture of a lovely horse, in all his splendid beauty. The pieces within the box, once opened and strewn across your table, are the separate bits that, when put together, make up the whole of what you see on the box cover.

Like the puzzle, your horse comes in two parts: the *physical* (the puzzle box) and the *emotional* (the puzzle pieces inside). When profiling for Emotional Confor-mation, I observe the horse to identify those unique pieces of the Individual Horse Personality (see chapter 2, p. 17). When fit together, the individual nuances, behav-ioral tendencies, Emergent Properties, and obvious behavioral dynamics, create a very unique profile of the equine psyche.

I must stress here that the Emotional Conformation Profile is *not* a tool for changing the horse—it is an indicator of his ability and potential. The horse is what the horse is, and Emotional Conformation goes far in unveiling that truth. The tools for change lie in your ability to train and compete the horse as best befits his mental aptitude—with the right goals identified, and the right methods used to pursue those goals, success will be the result.

6.2 A–K At the Pine Knoll Center for Integrated Horsemanship in Lexington, Kentucky, I introduce myself to Ballata, a lovely Lipizzaner, in order to begin to measure his Emotional Conformation (A). I am providing a basic emotional inspection to determine his suitability to be around people and his general trainability.

The first thing to determine is how big the horse's space is. When I find the distance where Ballata notices me, I pause so as not to push into his space, which can be viewed as threatening (B).

The space between me and the horse at this point is his. I'm "at the doorway" to the Equine Circle. The farther away I am when he acknowledges me, the bigger his Equine Circle is. The horse investigates those who enter the circle in stages, and this is a critical time. I make no sudden moves in this instant— change of posture can indicate a threat, and a knee-jerk reaction might be the result. I hold my position and let Ballata absorb my presence (C). He has transitioned from identifying a stimulus (me) to focusing on it. This is the moment of interpretation of intent.

When I identify a subtle alteration or transition in the horse, I need to respond to it in equally subtle posture changes, which display intent without overt action (D). Now I am beginning a dialogue. He should check me out, and then realize I am not a threat—notice his head has relaxed slightly. He passed the test. Once the dialogue is started, my avenue is opened to work and communicate—be it investigating Emotional Conformation or teaching/coaching the horse in some way.

Here I ask he share the space in front of him without threatening to take it (E). Note his ears are back but aloof as he at once defers and investigates. Body language reactions from the horse at this point indicate space issues. The horse's space should be tested from all sides—360 degrees.

I get low in front of Ballata—I like to use this line of sight because it is far less threatening than eye level (F).

6.2 A–K *continued* Because I am now pressing into his space subtly, I do not want it to be seen as a threat, but rather a curiosity to be investigated. Ballatta is showing good focus and interpretation of intentions. These are good earmarks for a potential therapy or family horse.

I next test his ability to release from space—once we have established our dialogue and the horse knows there is no threat, I like to break the focus the horse has on me. In this case handler Kao Fisher walks Ballata away (G). I stay in my crouched position to layer the positive response.

When Ballata turns back to me, I am where he left me (thus layering the acquired instinct—see p. 16). I expect him to "pick me up" and remember I am not a threat. Here, it is clear that he recognizes my presence and has no issue with moving back toward me (H). Ballata shows good retention. He is walking back to me softly, another good sign for a therapy or family horse.

As the distance between us decreases and the invisible line "connecting" us is locked, I rise to a standing position (I). He should be able to maintain

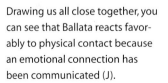

his focus on me and continue moving toward me without being bothered. His docile reaction means he is okay with me managing this space for him. How his pace is affected in this moment is an indicator of his Focus Agility (see p. 83).

Drawing us all close together, you can see that Ballata reacts favorably to physical contact because an emotional connection has been communicated (J).

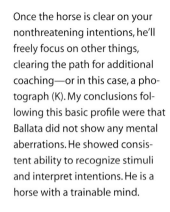

Once the horse is clear on your nonthreatening intentions, he'll freely focus on other things, clearing the path for additional coaching—or in this case, a photograph (K). My conclusions following this basic profile were that Ballata did not show any mental aberrations. He showed consistent ability to recognize stimuli and interpret intentions. He is a horse with a trainable mind.

P-Type Grading

Emotional Conformation is graded on two levels: *Personality Propensity Type* and *Potential*. This translates the behavioral dynamics of a horse into a letter grade and number that I refer to as the *P-Type*. Once you have a *P-Type* grade for a horse, you have a place to start in your quest to help him reach his fullest potential. The P-Type grade has a lot to do with *everything* your horse will encounter during his life. However, one P-Type is not necessarily *better than* another, nor does it necessarily

Kerry's Corner

Question: **For which purpose do you generally apply your theory of Emotional Conformation? What is the key use, or uses—or better put, what is the primary target area of focus when using it? I'm accepting of the concept but am seeking to make clear if I can make use of its application in my field of work.**
—Curious Consignor, Christchurch, New Zealand

Answer: I feel the very best way to answer this question regarding the *target areas of focus* of Emotional Conformation and P-Type grading is to essentially advance a general outline of the main areas to which they are most often applied:

Breeding/Mating Analysis: *Emergent Properties* of the female, identifiable as the Emotional Conformation within the *Group Herd Dynamic (GHD)* serve to advance and allow development of the latent *Now Properties* of the male, identifiable as the Emotional Conformation within the *Individual Herd Dynamic (IHD)*. GHD + IHD = foal tendencies. Nature knows best; this is why in a natural

environment it is primarily the female who selects her mate. Allowing the element of natural selection to be infused into the modern breeding program means a consideration of the Emotional Conformation of the proposed selections. (Read more about GHD and IHD beginning on p. 99.)

Pre-Purchase Evaluations: The added information provided by an evaluation that indicates Emotional Conformation and P-Type is invaluable and necessary in terms of investment decisions. As I have said, *the mental capacity of the equine controls the physical output of the athlete—* who is the pilot of that magnificent

airplane? Both active training and convalescence protocols can be designed to fit the *individual needs* of the horse with the help of an Emotional Conformation Profile. The individualized information revealed in the Emotional Conformation provides a solid foundation for the advancement of the horse in both his health and his competitive survival.

Informing the Rider/Jockey: Handing a horse's rider or jockey a psychological profile of the athlete he or she is about to board offers an intrepid training advancement and competitive edge. Nuances and other naturally occurring tendencies within the behavioral makeup of the horse can be readily identified and even anticipated. Knowing the depth of the horse's ability to focus and any number of other latent tendencies of the equine athlete helps raise a rider above and beyond others in the field that lack this knowledge of their own mounts.

indicate *greater leadership qualities* than another in a given situation or circumstance—it simply is manifested in different ways.

Personality Propensity Type

Personality Propensity Type reveals both the mental foundation and inner strengths of the individual horse and how those can best be used to *train forward,* expanding the horse's potential within the Equine Circle (fig. 6.3). The system utilizes a lower- and uppercase A and B to grade the horse's Personality Propensity Type.

- **a** = short-term *Focus Agility.* (Focus Agility is the horse's ability to focus on stimuli while in motion, including how the horse handles the stimuli—correct diagnosis of threat/nonthreat—and how that diagnosis affects the horse's pace. In other words, it is his ability to mentally and physically multitask.) Indicates the primary ability to focus is strongest over a short *time-in-motion* (physical energy plus emotional energy equals time-in-motion—see chapter 8, p. 105, for more about this). For example: focus required for sprinting, roping, reining, cutting, and polo, where the horse is required to be athletic in powerful, short bursts and respond to quick knee-jerk commands from the rider. When used in conjunction with **A** this P-Type indicates the dual propensity of both short to medium Focus Agility. For example: **aA** indicates a primary sprinter who may be advanced to perform over middle distances.

- **A** = moderate levels of Focus Agility. Indicates the primary Focus Agility is strongest over a short to medium time-in-motion—for example: a sprinter with the ability to stretch out to a mile. Barrel racing and roping horses who perform at a high level are often graded out to be ideal **A** P-Type horses. I have also found that hunter-jumpers of both **A** and **b** P-Typing (see below) are able to elevate their physical athletic ability nicely. P-Type **A** horses are generally faster to mature mentally, where P-Type **B** horses (see p. 84) are often slower to develop mentally, but eventually have the ability to focus with confidence over a longer period of time-in-motion.

- **Ab** = mid-level or average Focus Agility. An example in the Thoroughbred would be a classic miler. If you are looking for the all-around good and semi-versatile equine athlete, the kind of horse you might use for combined driving events or be able to enjoy on a moderately challenging trail ride, you're looking for the **Ab** P-Type. This is the overwhelming *herd average* equine mind, and should *not* be confused with the *simple mind.* Horses with this P-Type are generally flexible in various ways and for various uses, not too strong and not too weak. Whatever their physical ability or body type, the **Ab** mental aptitude is usually good in any given task.

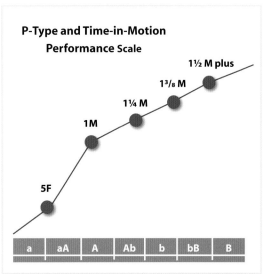

P-Type and Time-in-Motion Performance Scale

1½ M plus

1³/₈ M

1¼ M

1M

5F

| a | aA | A | Ab | b | bB | B |

6.3 Although this chart was designed for evaluating distance aptitude in Thoroughbred racehorses (F = furlong, M = mile), the P-Types (along the horizontal axis) apply to all equine athletes. For example, high-level prospects for dressage, eventing, or endurance competition need to fall into the P-Type bB or higher (further right). As demonstrated by the distances well-handled at certain levels on the scale, a trainable mind and the ability to focus over an extended period of time-in-motion is necessary to achieve lofty goals in any of these more demanding equestrian sports.

- **b** = above-average Focus Agility. When used in conjunction with **B**, indicates the dual propensity of medium Focus Agility and protracted time-in-motion—for example: **bB** might be a primary router (in racing, a horse that prefers distances of a mile or longer) with ability for middle distance. Other equine athletes that excel in the b range are dressage horses. In fact 90 percent of upper level dressage horses I have profiled or spent any time with have graded out to P-Type **b**. I have also found that a great majority of the best equine-assisted therapy horses fall into this category. (Note: Focus Agility is the determining factor that allows a horse to efficiently manage his time-in-motion. Thus the signature marker for distance aptitude is any P-Type **b** and above.)

- **B** = a protracted and naturally well-developed Focus Agility. Indicates the primary ability to focus develops over a more protracted time-in-motion—for example: focus required for long distances (over a mile in racing). I have found steeplechase mounts, endurance competitors, and some show horses that are at a high level of mental soundness fit into this P-Type. (Note: **b** and **B** P-Types are in the zone of what I personally identify as the most trainable equine mind.)

- **+** = above average.

- **-** = below average.

Potential Level

Potential Level represents the individual horse's overall likelihood of improving in a given area of the Equine Circle, such as in training, breeding, or performing.

- **(1–5)** = the level of potential, with 1 being lowest.

- **(d)** = the potential is a *developmental prospect,* such as when profiling a foal or weanling.

- **(f)** = the potential as a *foundation prospect,* such as when profiling a stallion or a mare for a breeding program.

- **+** = above average.

- **-** = below average.

Avoiding Stereotyping

In any group of horses you will find various personality strengths and weakness exposed in the ways they react to or communicate with other horses and their environment. If your horse seems to think he needs to impress his physical self upon a space, even in the subtlest of ways, as opposed to his buddy, who simply makes his presence felt by "just being there," you have two different types of horses. The "markers" you can use to begin to profile your own horse are found squarely within the ways in which the two communicate. This is important, because it isn't just *the information that is given but the way in which the information given is delivered*—that is the governing factor of understanding what your horse is "saying" and what he is "being told." If you want to develop a proper training program for your equine athlete, you need to know the ways in which your horse interprets and translates communication between himself and other horses, and between himself and humans.

The pedigree of the dressage horse may show that the family bloodline is one with remarkable physical ability but a tendency to be inconsistent in competition. An Emotional Conformation

P-Type Profile Examples

P-Type A(3+) is a horse with a sprinter's mental capacity and focus level, with an average ability to be elevated. (*Potential* of 3+ means that the horse has a basic to good ability to be *trained forward.*) If I were working a herd of cattle, or heading off to play a game of polo, or leaving the scene of (my) bank robbery in the Old West, my A(3+) horse would be my ride of choice.

P-Type aA(d) indicates a short to medium Focus Agility in the *developmental prospect*—so suitable for *training forward* with an eye toward increased Focus Agility.

P-Type ab(3) indicates an equine athlete with moderate Focus Agility and average potential to be *trained forward*—for example, in racing, a classic miler.

P-Type B(3+) is the horse with a distance athlete's mental capacity and focus level. He can manage stimuli and hold concentration over a long period of time and distance, and displays an average to slightly above-average potential. Horses with this mental aptitude are better achievers.

P-Type B(f) indicates a foundation breeding prospect with a strong protracted Focus Agility.

Profile can indicate whether or not the horse has the mental capacity and trainable mind that would allow his remarkable physical ability to ever truly excel in the ring. While the pedigree of the Thoroughbred may suggest he is best suited for sprinting, an Emotional Conformation Profile can show if he has the potential to be competitive in longer races. Conversely, the opposite may be true—the pedigree may show that a horse could be a good router while an Emotional Conformation Profile indicates he is actually best suited to sprints or middle distance races. The Emotional Conformation Profile allows you to establish training protocols and competitive strategy that will help your current horse reach his full potential, and help you buy and breed horses suited to reaching your competitive goals—be that in the dressage ring, the reining show pen, or on the racetrack.

Our friend Federico Tesio knew the importance of not "stereotyping" the horse (according to his pedigree) and instead allowing the horse to live up to his full potential (according to his character). Of Tesio's racehorses, Nearco—a stallion found in the pedigree of many of today's elite event horses and jumpers the world over—was one of his greatest, and yet, Tesio believed that Nearco was not a true "stayer," in the classic sense (capable of running over longer distances). From birth, however, Nearco possessed a keenness of mind or nervous energy, an Emergent Property that Tesio embraced and used to train Nearco forward. By nurturing that nervous energy

Kerry's Corner

Question: **I have one very good horse in training, but we seem to be at a crossroads. Can you use your P-Type technique to help me determine if my horse has hit a mental wall, or if we need to tweak his training program to open the door so his mental capacity can match his obvious physical ability?**
—Thoroughbred Owner, Kentucky, United States

Answer: One of the unique aspects and uses of P-Type grading is the determination of the mental capacity, and moreover the Emotional Conformation, of the horse. This is extremely relevant information for so many things—ongoing training and training protocols designed to match the athlete to the appropriate task high among them. P-Type offers a unique and powerful insight to the equine psyche. It allows you to get to know and understand your horse as an individual, opening the door to the development of training standards specifically designed for your *individual* horse's needs. The *mental* demands of the in-training equine athlete require as much nurturing as the physical. Developing both the mind and body of any athlete is vitally important in order to reach his highest potential. No matter how majestic looking the within, rather than attempting to quell it, Tesio turned Nearco into an undefeated champion, and the horse finished his racing career by winning the 12-furlong (1½ mile) Grand Prix de Paris—one of the most prestigious races in France.

Like Tesio, knowing how to expand on what is *inherent,* and often hidden, means getting the most from your horse without compromising *your goals* or the *welfare of the horse.* Emotional Conformation Profiling allows the horse owner to find the areas that need the most nurturing, and thus confidence and potential increases.

Applying an Emotional Conformation Profile

The Emotional Conformation Profile becomes highly efficacious for many avenues, from pre-purchase exams to breeding plans, as it is an immediate indicator of the psychological makeup of the horse. The P-Type grade is a powerful tool to have in your shed because it is information that adds value to your equine investment— whether you already own it, are looking to purchase it, or are planning breeding lines or training protocols.

One of the ways profiling can benefit the equine athlete is when the profile is used as a cornerstone for the development of an individual *playbook,* designed to elevate the *"who"* into *"what could be."* Mentally nurturing your horse is vitally

airplane, you still need a pilot who can get the most out of it.

Determining if *there is more in the tank* that can be tapped with a little nurturing here and there, or whether your athlete has simply *reached his potential* and no amount of training physically will change the outcome, plays an important role in the decision-making process as regards what is best for the horse. The inconsistent athlete

may be fraught with latent variables creating *Potential Withholds* (see p. 125), which inhibit progress. Or it may well be that, essentially, *this is it,* and to continue to press a square peg into a round hole will end up in disappointment and perhaps even injury.

P-Type helps to sort out this puzzle and provides powerful information that can be applied to the ongoing training process

by monitoring progress, potential, overall sustainable capacity, and ability to focus. Essentially the question that needs to be answered via an Emotional Conformation Profile is: does the athlete have a trainable mind so as to get the most efficiency from his physical conformation? The mental soundness of the horse will in the end be your governing factor.

important for overall health and success. An Emotional Conformation Profile of the horse can go a long way in your decision-making process when forming or revising training regimens and honing competitive strategy. (We'll examine training the equine athlete in chapter 8, beginning on p. 105.) A profile of the in-training athlete is also an asset when seeking to find ways to elevate above a performance plateau or work through *Potential Withholds* (see p. 125) by finding the *sweet spot*—that comfort zone that "releases" your horse's true ability.

An Emotional Conformation Profile can answer the myriad questions one often has when working with horses: Should my horse go into training? Should he be pushed harder? Should he have some time off? Should my mare be used as a broodmare? What is the best way to maintain my horse's mental health while he is recovering from injury? How do I keep my horse happy when shipping him long distances? Should I buy this horse? And so on.

The main goal of Emotional Conformation Profiling is to help bring the horse into focus. In the end, the more you know about your horse, the better your relationship will be—and it really matters not what the goals are for that relationship.

7 Discovering the Communicated Equine

"You must endeavor to understand, before you seek to be understood."

The next crucial step on our journey is to learn how to discover what I call the *Communicated Equine.* The domestic horse, much like his cousins in the wild, relies on a communication dynamic in order to establish herd hierarchy. Herd animals that travel in close proximity have to be able to comprehend the intentions of the other "moving parts" of the group—some defer, others impress their will in subtle, nearly automatic transfers of control over space. Knowing how the individual horse will react within the herd is the key to his proper management. Once you have measured your equine athlete's Emotional Conformation, you need to understand the communication dynamic in order to establish successful training protocols for him.

Communication Is Key to Survival and Success

The ability to communicate, and do it well, is a key ingredient for the success and survival of all living creatures. If you watch bees working in a beehive or ants gathering food for the colony, you are keenly aware of an unseen, yet highly sophisticated, communication network that governs their actions. In human endeavors, such as the world of high-powered business, successful communicators grow and expand to become corporate giants, while the unsuccessful communicators go bankrupt.

In the Equine Circle, the dynamic of a sophisticated communication network is evident when you observe a herd at rest suddenly begin to move to a new location—be it simply to a new feeding ground or to a place where the herd is safe from predators. The herd's survival depends on communication, and horses are good communicators; however, how they do it is not easily perceptible to the human eye (fig. 7.1).

The Concealed Leader

Mother Nature is sneaky when it comes to nurturing survival of the herd, and one of the methods she uses to ensure that survival is to conceal communication between the lead horse and other horses in the herd. Why is this so? Because the herd has better chances of survival if a low- or middle-level horse is lost to predators instead of the leader. Often the lead horse is concealed within the herd when it is at rest. Sometimes the lead horse will also hide within the herd if he or she feels threatened or there is a communication breakdown among the other horses. The lead horse is more discernible when the herd roams across prairies and meadows.

In the domestic environment, the lead horse is also not necessarily recognizable—although mostly because many domestic "herds" spend most of their time cooped up in stalls. Nevertheless, the hierarchy is the same: all of the horses in the barn know the lead horse, and with only subtle persuasion, they give way when that horse walks by—and this rule applies on the racetrack and in the show ring. To add complexity to the scenario, the lead horse can also be "concealed" from the "human predator," and thus quietly hidden before our very eyes, and indeed, quite often overlooked (fig. 7.2).

How the hierarchy is established and communication is transmitted within the herd is vital for the herd's survival. The ability to comprehend the working of this communication network within the herd is essential for your success as a trainer because it allows you to properly communicate your goals or *intentions* to the horses in your training program. But how does one bridge the communication gap between human and horse?

An Emotional Conformation Profile of the horses in your stable will give a clear picture of where every horse fits into the

7.1 A lead mare leads a young colt toward a new feeding ground and stream in the Bighorn Mountains. The mare is aware of what is going on in front of her, but her ears are back, surveying what is behind her. She is trying to "drag" a line of horses along (there are more horses out of frame to the right). She knows the closer the herd gets to the water source, the greater the chance of attack from predators. She is encouraging the herd to tighten up, so there are no stragglers or easy targets.

herd hierarchy (see more about this beginning on p. 94). As you learned in the last two chapters, Emotional Conformation Profiling identifies the singular aspects of a horse's ability to comprehend and communicate environmental stimuli. The lower your horse is on the P-Type Scale (see fig. 6.3, p. 84), the lower he is in *Herd Dynamic*—his position on the herd "totem pole." Higher P-Types (**Ab** and above) hold higher positions in the herd or have the potential to advance. The reason for this is that the ability to focus, communicate, and interpret stimuli are integral both for leadership and survival in the wild. Sprint horses with limited focus ability (P-Type **A**) are the ones who never "elevate" to positions of herd leadership, and they are likely to be the first to be culled by predators. The majority of horses fall into the middle range (P-Type **Ab**).

The next step is to gain an understanding of the communication dynamics that occur within a particular herd. What works with each horse in the herd can help you establish training protocols that best suit the individual behavioral dynamic of each horse in your stable.

7.2 Horses can show leadership from any position, including from behind the pack. Thoroughbred champion Zenyatta (#4, in last place) is an example of the highest Group Herd Dynamic (see p. 99). From her position at the back of the pack in the 2009 Breeders' Cup Classic at Santa Anita Park in California, she is able to identify the intentions and movements of all the other horses. Although the human sees Zenyatta in last place, Zenyatta sees herself in a position to manage her "herd."

The Dialects of Equine Communication

Equine communication consists of two *dialects*—body language and intent. *Body language* is the basic and most universal form of communication used by all horses. *Intent* is a more subtle form of body language and the highest form of communication expressed by higher level herd horses. Horses that primarily communicate with intent need only minimal accompanying body-language accents (or often none at all) to influence other horses while the herd is on the move or at rest. Such horses have a "presence" that enables them to convey their intentions and have them fully understood and respected with just a look, a twitch of an ear, a brief gesture.

A good example of how herd leaders and high-level horses (see p. 94) communicate with intent comes to us from Federico Tesio, who tells the story of an experience he had as a young man while driving a herd of horses with gauchos on the Argentine Pampas in *Breeding the Racehorse:*

> At times not a breath of air stirred the grass of the prairie as far as the eye could reach. Suddenly a horse would prick up his ears, paw the ground and lie down. Within a few minutes every horse in the herd would follow suit. What is more, they would all lie with their backs turned in the same direction. It would not be long before the first gusts of the "Pampero" would be upon us, blowing from that very direction. The Pampero is a violent wind-storm, fiercer even than the "Bora" of Trieste, and when it blows it is next to impossible to stand upright.

Tesio did not have an explanation for the behavior of the horses, and he speculated that it was perhaps due to a sixth sense they possessed. But, his story is a perfect example of how herd leaders communicate and lead with the dialect of intent. In my study of the wild horse, I had similar experiences. One that sticks in my mind occurred during a research trip in 2008 to the Bighorn Mountains.

Bearing Witness to the Communication of Intent

It was a windy day as I meandered my way around scrub oaks and sage to a vantage point atop a butte overlooking an area called Mustang Flats. For several days atop the butte, I had observed a small herd that consisted of a stallion, two mares, a young colt, and two fillies. When I got to my observation post, I spotted the herd on the flats below. The stallion kept vigil over his band from a distance of about 25 yards while the mares watched over the colt and fillies that were playing around as young horses often do. The behavior of the herd was much the same that day as I had observed on previous occasions.

After a while, the wind died down and an indescribable stillness that one can only experience in the West, far removed from the hustle and bustle of city life, enveloped the flats. This kind of stillness is my favorite time to get "in tune" with Mother Nature and the environment. All your senses are heightened in the stillness, and it was at such a moment that I realized something was different about the herd. The stallion who had stood at a distance now started to slowly move in a round-about fashion around the herd. The lead mare, who had been reclining, rose to her feet and fixed her gaze on the stallion. The other mare with ears pricked and slight body language took a position beside the young fillies and colt who had stopped their play and were frozen in their tracks. The communication network amongst the herd was mesmerizing and nearly indiscernible.

The stallion, still maintaining his distance, was now a bit closer and on the opposite side of the herd from where he originally stood vigil. The mare that stood by the young horses slowly started to walk away while the young horses followed in her path. The lead mare joined the procession at the rear, casually leading the young ones from the back of the herd as they made their way over the flats until they were out of sight. The stallion lingered long enough to be sure there were no immediate threats and to make certain that none of the young horses strayed away. Satisfied that the herd was safe, the stallion slowly disappeared out of sight.

What I had witnessed was a perfect example of a lead stallion communicating with his dialect of intent to move his herd from their place of rest. Lead horses will lead from any position they feel is required to perpetuate proper herd motion. If they are leading to water or food, they mostly lead from the front or near it. However, in cases where danger may be present, lead horses will position themselves between the herd underlings and the perceived threat. This behavior is similar to that of other herd animals across the planet—for example, African water buffalo encircle calves when lions approach.

I searched the terrain with my binoculars to see if any predators were present, but I did not see any. I waited about an hour to make sure that the herd was well out of sight before descending from my observation post to the flats below. In the wild, and even when preparing Emotional Conformation Profiles, I always try to be the unobtrusive observer of the horse in his environment. However, the wild herd had been spooked, and I was I was determined to find out why. About 75 yards out along a horse path that led to where the herd was when I first spotted them, I discovered a fresh set of mountain lion tracks, and although I had not seen the predator, the stallion had been keenly aware of its presence. The intimate drama of life in the Equine Circle had played out before my very eyes. Mother Nature in her infinite wisdom and the stallion with his subtle dialect of intent had ensured survival of the herd for another day.

Communication Chain-of-Command

The Equine Circle, which I introduced in chapter 2 (p. 13), consists of five *hierarchy levels:* low, mid, adjunct, high, and herd leader. Members of each level communicate with the others using various forms of body language and intent in a chain-of-

Dynamics of the Herd— The Fabric of Life

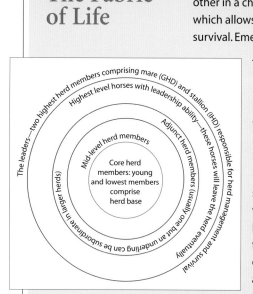

7.3 The equine herd chain-of-command.

The body of the equine herd is generally made up of five layers (fig. 7.3). Each layer communicates with the other in a chain-of-command structure, which allows for optimum efficiency and survival. Emerging members of the herd jostle for position almost daily in sometimes subtle, sometimes lavish displays of body language and infractions of space.

The base of the herd (the center of the diagram) is comprised of the lowest-standing members, along with the youngest. The next layer (working your way out from the center) is made up of mid-level horses who are always at risk to challenges of position from the base members—thus these first two layers can be flip-flopped at any given moment and any number of times. About 80 percent of horses fall into these two categories.

The next level horse is a key member of the herd—the adjunct horse. Because of this horse's position and unique ability to communicate fluently with both intent and body language, he is commonly but falsely recognized as the herd leader. The job of the adjunct is to act as liaison between the lead horses and the rest of the herd members, especially when the group is in motion. Adjunct horses rarely seek or desire to "move up" in herd hierarchy.

Above the adjunct and just below the actual herd leaders are high-level herd members who have only one role—waiting. They play little or no part in herd motion unless challenging the current lead stallion or mare for top position. When the lead position is unattainable, high-level horses are either pushed out of their "vice-presidency" to start their own herd, move into bachelor herds, or continue to lay in waiting for an older or infirmed leader eventually to give way.

command structure, which allows for optimum efficiency and survival. Emerging members of the herd jostle for position almost daily in sometimes subtle, sometimes lavish displays of body language and infractions of space. A family herd generally is made up of four to seven members at any given moment, but circumstances, of course, dictate actual numbers.

The core or *base* of the herd is comprised of the young and the *lowest-level horses*. The next herd group is *mid-level horses* who are always at risk to challenges of position from the base members—80 percent of the herd consists of the lower and mid-level behavioral categories. Body language is the primary method of communication expressed by horses in the lower and mid-level behavioral groups. At the top of the mid-level herd group is the *adjunct horse,* who is a vital link for communication between the high-level horse and the low-level horses. The next group in the chain-of-command consists of *high-level horses* and *herd leaders.* High-level horses are capable of communicating with body language and intent. However, intent is their primary means of communication, and this allows them to communicate with the herd without exposing themselves to dangerous predators.

Low-Level Horses

Horses at the lower end of the Herd Dynamic express themselves far more overtly to impact their space or to exert their command over other horses and even their handlers. Humans often mistake this combative, expressive behavior as a sign that the horse possesses qualities of authority and leadership, when most often, that is not the case. When a horse reacts immediately and violently, pushing you away from his space, it should be considered a sign of insecurity. Such behavior reveals that the horse may have had a bad experience when previously handled or that he is simply not at all interested in you and your training program. This reaction can also be a clear sign of a communication breakdown.

Lower herd members have difficulty recognizing the quiet, intent-based language of the leaders, who use very little noticeable body language to convey their message. The lowest members of the herd use body language much of the time and often expose their insecurity by the way they react to stimuli, as mentioned, either pressing violently into space or reacting in a fear-tainted aggressive manner to space infractions. Because they struggle to fully understand the dialect of intent, lower level horses struggle to gain positions of power. This said, *all* horses can learn enough to elevate to a higher standing within the herd, even though, depending on the size of the herd, they may have to bide their time or fight it out with others seeking to climb higher in the hierarchy. (Many great equine athletes can be found and developed within this group if this is kept in mind.)

The low-level horse:

- Uses body language as the primary form of communication.

- Is space-protective out of insecurity more than out of desire to manage and control a space. (This is an action, not a *reaction.*)

- Is more inclined to force himself into the space of another horse, human, or anything he finds threatening to his own space.

- Is more likely to knee-jerk react to sudden or unexpected environmental stimuli.

- Has a great deal of difficulty understanding anything but concise body language from humans or horses.

What to Remember When Working with the Low-Level Horse

Horses low in herd hierarchy are good at short bursts of energy. They can be very athletic animals, but they need to be targeted for tasks with a confined timeframe, and they need to be directed by a skilled rider.

Mid-Level and Adjunct Horses

Playful engagement is a signature of mid-level group members and is prevalent in the male. The mid-level horse is fun, easy, endearing of character, and we grow fond of him. At times, an overly gregarious form of communication is found, predominantly in what I refer to as the *adjunct horse,* who serves as the translator or communicator of information from the lead horse to other horses in the herd, especially when the herd is in motion. This horse's body language is expressive but not necessarily combative. He has a better ability to gauge the intent of other horses in the herd and also seeks physical engagement.

The adjunct horse occupies the top tier of the mid-level herd group. Because of this horse's position and unique ability to communicate fluently with both body language and intent, he is the most commonly but falsely recognized as the herd leader. Adjunct horses rarely seek or desire to move up, a quality vital for herd survival as the adjunct horse is the primary source of communication to other horses lower in the hierarchy. As, in effect, the herd "translator," the adjunct horse is adept at extracting information from intent or body language and conveying that information to other horses. In many ways, the "translator" is the most important communicator in the herd.

The mid-level and adjunct horse:

- Can be at various levels of his education in herd social life.

- Has a wide array of communication styles.

- Can rely on body language as a primary means of communication when at the lower end of the mid-level spectrum, but is beginning to learn how to recognize the language of intent.

- Uses less forced body language to express or to react to others and to stimuli but is still prone to sudden outbursts.

What to Remember When Working with the Mid-Level and Adjunct Horse
Mid-level horses make up the body of the herd. They are good at a lot of things. They are relatively trainable because they generally don't question or make demands. They make wonderful pleasure-riding horses or companions. Mid-level horses *can* be good competitors, but they are limited to their physical abilities and are unlikely to succeed at the highest level of most equestrian disciplines.

Adjunct horses are among my favorites. The adjunct is what I call the "great communicator" because of his ability to communicate with everyone, from the highest to lowest members of the herd. Adjunct horses are the very best dressage horses and also are great equine-assisted therapy horses because of their high-level communication skills. Adjuncts also have the mental ability to excel athletically.

High-Level Horses and Herd Leaders
Above the adjunct and just below the actual herd leaders are high-level herd members who have only one role—waiting for an older or infirm leader to eventually give way. (Herd leaders are simply high-level horses who assumed the highest ranking position in the group.) High-level horses play little or no part in herd motion unless challenging the current lead stallion or mare for top position. If this position is unattainable, they will eventually either be pushed out to start their own herd or move into bachelor herds. Thus a leadership structure is always maintained.

Leaderless herds are not in nature's design. High dynamic horses, especially males, have a stealth-like character to them, and this is a positive trait that should be considered when seeking sires for a breeding program.

The high-level horse and herd leader:

- Understands and has the best command over all of the dialects and accents of equine language.

- Rarely reacts with body language unless deemed necessary and has a *presence* about him, allowing him to manage the herd from a distance.

- Communicates almost exclusively with other high-level and mid-level horses. (In normal conditions, the mid-level acts as the communicator to other horses in the herd.)

- May often seem aloof, disinterested, and go unnoticed—part of nature's design to conceal herd leaders.

Equine Dialect Communication Levels

Communication between the various hierarchal levels of the herd is the key to survival. The differentiating factor between the levels of individual horses within the herd unit rests within the individual's capacity to communicate either via intent or body language—or both. Intent is the highest form of communication needing only minimal or often no accompanying body-language accents to influence other horses. Therefore, horses higher on the "totem pole" demonstrate greater fluency in the dialect of intent, as well as the dialect of body language (fig. 7.4).

As noted on the chart, *both* primary *and* secondary dialects of communication for the various levels of the herd play a key role between members, while allowing for structure and a distinct chain-of-command. Identifying the communication dialect of the equine athlete is the first step toward a deeper understanding of his strengths and weaknesses. The ability to communicate, and to comprehend what is being communicated, is a singular piece of the behavioral puzzle that can either inhibit mental growth and learning or elevate the horse to a higher level in the herd hierarchy—and to greater success in the show ring or on the racetrack.

7.4 Primary and secondary forms of communication according to herd level.

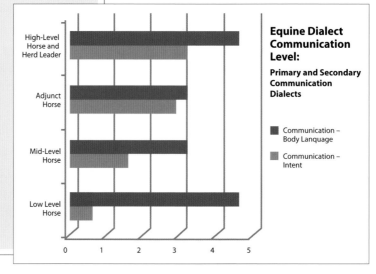

Equine Dialect Communication Level:

Primary and Secondary Communication Dialects

- Communication – Body Language
- Communication – Intent

- Will sometimes steer clear of lower-level horses for fear of being targeted by proximity of space.

What to Remember When Working with a High-Level Horse or Herd Leader
High-level horses have the ability to achieve the highest athletic goals humans can set for them. They also require specific training because they get bored easily. High-level horses are "thinkers" and tremendously advanced communicators, but they can be stubborn. They are the best racing, endurance, and eventing horses, but they must be physically trained and mentally nurtured.

Herd Dynamics

The *Natural Herd Dynamic* is the everyday behavior and interaction that occurs within the intricate social order of herd hierarchies within the Equine Circle. The communication between individual herd members allows for growth and survival as each member of the herd is interested in *self-preservation,* as well as *herd preservation.* This preservation instinct is manifested in what I call the *Individual Herd Dynamic* and *Group Herd Dynamic.* The higher the horse is positioned in herd hierarchy level, the better able he is to express these communication dynamics.

Individual Herd Dynamic

The Individual Herd Dynamic is most often expressed by stallions in the herd. A stallion's primary focus is on *individual needs,* which are self-serving. His role in the herd is to target space, individuals, threats, competition, and breeding prospects. His job as a leader is to protect and manage his herd environment by keeping stragglers in line and threats at bay.

Male herd members are usually 70 percent focused on Individual Herd Dynamics and 30 percent Group Herd Dynamics (see p. 100). This allows the horse to manage and govern from a distance, which is required to maintain vigil over the herd and recognize individual targets, whether within or without the group as a whole. In other words, he will target any individual thing, friend or foe, that may negatively impact him or the group.

High Level Individual Herd Dynamic Indicators

Self-awareness
Space management
Targeted intent to control body language
Controlled anticipation and target-and-release ability
Aloofness to nonthreatening space violations
"Presence" of character and silent leadership
Ability to influence at variable ranges

Testing for Individual Herd Dynamic

Equine athletes should be evaluated with the Individual Herd Dynamic in mind. Perform the following tests to detect behavioral indicators of the Individual Herd Dynamic:

- Observe your horse in a herd and identify the distance of space around him that is both influencing his own movement and reactions, and that of others.

- Observe the earmarks of the herd's communication. Is your horse using overt body language for his base form of delivering a message? Is he reacting to *what is said* or does it appear he is reacting to *what he's interpreting,* with body language as his primary means of communication?

- Does your horse seem to depend on a "buddy" to translate information for him? Or does he make what appears to be concise and smooth transitions based on his own observations and interpretations? (Note: This is important to note when you're communicating with your horse and when you're gauging how fast to add mental challenges to his training regime.)

Group Herd Dynamic

The Group Herd Dynamic is primarily expressed by female herd members who have a naturally occurring mothering, nurturing attitude toward their social group. High-level mares have the ability to read the intentions and Emergent Properties of all the other herd members, and their job is to guard and protect the welfare of the group as a whole—especially when the herd is in motion. When the herd is in motion, high-level mares are keenly aware of the other herd members and have the ability manage and guide the herd in any direction.

Testing for Group Herd Dynamic

Watch for the following characteristics of Group Herd Dynamics in your horses:

- Observe your horse in a herd. The horse with a high Group Herd Dynamic has the ability to be comfortable in group environments without overt indicators or stress.

High Level Group Herd Dynamic Indicators

Total herd or group awareness

Ability to monitor group by reading all members' intent at a given moment

Toleration and nurturing of individual group members

Communicates almost exclusively with intent

Manages herd motion by leading or directing space

- Notice whether your horse has the ability to negotiate multiple stimuli and maintain focus.

- Determine whether the horse can manage the space of more than one horse, primarily by recognizing the other horses' intentions.

- Note if the horse is able to communicate with little use of body language accents. The use of overt body language should be a playful choice and not the horse's primary form of communication.

7.5 A–C Thoroughbred sire Hat Trick, a son of champion Thoroughbred Sunday Silence, has one of the highest Herd Dynamics that I have seen in a horse. This was our first meeting, at Walmac Farm near Lexington, Kentucky, in January 2011 (A).

What the Individual and Group Herd Dynamic Mean in the Sport Horse

The horse with a predominantly Individual Herd Dynamic (mostly a male trait) is more likely to individualize his targets and stimuli. Equine athletes with a high Individual Herd Dynamic need to be taught to transition from goal to goal, as opposed to targeting just one focus point (such as another competitor on the track, for example). The horse with a strong Individual Herd Dynamic can be a very effective equine-assisted therapy horse for a rider with a single particular condition or challenge.

The horse with a stronger Group Herd Dynamic (usually a female trait) is good at interpreting multiple stimuli within an environment. This horse embraces the "larger picture" much more efficiently than a horse with a dominant Individual Herd Dynamic.

High Group Herd Dynamic horses need to be taught what to do with the information they are so good at processing. For example, the high Group Herd Dynamic racehorse needs to be taught when to make a move and how to lead from a forward position (such horses are often content with leading from behind).

The horse with a strong Group Herd Dynamic horse is a good candidate for any athletic task that takes place within an environment that contains a lot of chaos or stimuli, such as a show pen or an arena in front of a large, noisy crowd. He can also be a very good equine-assisted therapy horse for riders with multiple challenges.

CASE STUDIES

Three of the best examples of exceptional horses I have met who are "Communicated Equines" are racing Thoroughbreds: Hat Trick, Zenyatta, and Animal Kingdom.

7.5 A–C *continued* The stallion sized me up—note his right ear is forward while his left ear keeps tabs on what is going on behind him (B). Just like a stallion in the wild, Hat Trick was able to investigate new stimuli while remaining completely aware of his surroundings. After he investigated me, he returned to his role as the seemingly aloof, quiet leader (C).

These horses operate at the highest levels of Herd Dynamics.

Hat Trick

In January of 2011, during a visit to Kentucky, I had the opportunity to see the sire Hat Trick, who was standing stud at Walmac Farm (figs. 7.5 A–C). Hat Trick has the strongest Individual Herd Dynamic I have ever seen, and one of the highest Group Herd Dynamics, as well. Hat Trick also displayed one of the most subtly powerful communication abilities I have ever seen in a horse. His behavioral characteristics are the qualities I look for in a first-class sire prospect. What I mean by all this is that upon first seeing Hat Trick, I didn't need to study his personality, his management of his environment, or interpret any stimulus research to "know" who he was. He had a stealth-like character that is indicative of high-level herd horses, and from far off, I could *feel* his presence.

Hat Trick's first runners went to the racetrack in 2011 and the best runner from his first foal crop of was Dabirsim. As a two-year-old racing in France, Dabirsim was undefeated in five starts, winning three group races and becoming the Cartier Racing Awards European Champion. Given a chance, Hat Trick can be successful at stud. It remains to be seen if breeders will key in to his potential, as they overlooked his sire Sunday Silence when *he* went to stud.

Zenyatta

In the summer of 2009, THT business manager Larry Knepper and I, along with filmmaker Amanda Roxborough of Kylar Products, went to Hollywood Park in Inglewood, California, to film me profiling horses. It wasn't long after we arrived and were watching horses being schooled in the paddock that I noticed a mare among a group of six or seven horses. At the time, I had no idea what Zenyatta looked like, but my instinct told me that this particular horse was Zenyatta. I later discovered I was right.

7.6 Having assumed the forward leadership role approaching the finish line of the 2009 Breeders' Cup Classic, Zenyatta continues to manage and control what is behind her while maintaining a forward focus (left ear cocked forward).

My thoughts upon seeing Zenyatta were much the same as my first impression of Hat Trick. I could feel her presence from the other side of the paddock—I've sensed that before studying high-level horses in the wild. Watching Zenyatta in the paddock was like observing a natural herd leader in complete command of her environment. I've mentioned that nature conceals herd leaders, and this applies to Zenyatta—in some ways she was inconspicuous among the other horses but her Herd Dynamic and ability to communicate was so high that she was in complete command of all the other horses around her. It was obvious Zenyatta was impacting the other horses because *they* were reacting to *her* presence. Great horses *impact and influence* far more than they are impacted or influenced. It was the silent power Zenyatta displayed in her actions and intentions that defined her (fig. 7.6). Two days later, trainer John Shirreffs graciously allowed us an opportunity to visit with Zenyatta.

Animal Kingdom

Often, the only means I have to prepare an Emotional Conformation Profile is to watch film footage of a horse—I do this often for prospective clients. Such was the case in April of 2011 when I was approached by turf writer Pete Denk who was writing a story about profiling the horses entered in the Kentucky Derby for the online magazine *Kentucky Confidential*. I liked the idea and agreed to the project.

Over the next few days, after watching hours of film footage of the horses slated to participate in the Kentucky Derby, I saw several horses with various time-in-

7.7 2011 Kentucky Derby winner Animal Kingdom exhibits a powerful, into-space motion even while both ears reach back to feel the horses behind him. An example of a very high Individual Herd Dynamic, Animal Kingdom was able to move and manage the space of other horses.

motion issues, such as "buddy up," where a horse runs neck-and-neck with another horse in the race—be it at the lead, in the middle, or at the end of the herd. Other horses had behavioral overcompensation issues (see p. 141) because of the blinkers they wore. But one of the few standouts from the proposed field was Animal Kingdom, who displayed very high-level abilities in both Individual and Group Herd Dynamics and was always in self-control (fig. 7.7).

Animal Kingdom had a very powerful running style, and one of the earmarks I look for when film profiling is how well equine athletes manage stimuli while in motion. *Patterns of motion* and *patterns of behavior* are reciprocal mirrors, one to the other. Even though I didn't get to see Animal Kingdom in person until *after* the Derby when he came back to Fair Hill Training Center in Maryland, what I saw in calm moments on film was clearly what I saw when he was in motion. What stood out was his seemingly natural ability to manage multiple stimuli while in motion, which led me to believe his presence, which at times seemed to "part the seas" in a race, would be an impressive one.

In the performances I saw on film, Animal Kingdom showed all the earmarks of an athlete on the move forward with the mental ability to get the most from his physical capacity. He, frankly, stood out from the other horses in the Derby field. In assessing the Emotional Conformation Profile of Animal Kingdom, it wasn't too difficult to predict that his presence in the nineteen-horse field would have an influence over the other "herd members," and that he was a good pick to win.

8 Training the Equine Athlete

"You are training for time-in-motion, making Emotional Conformation and Focus Agility of essential importance."

Now that you have discovered the Communicated Equine, the next step is to apply what have you learned: evaluate the horses in your stable to determine where they fit in hierarchy of the Equine Circle. An Emotional Conformation Profile and P-Type grade (see chapter 6, p. 78) enables you to identify the high-level horses with a strong Herd Dynamic and a potentially "trainable mind"—and those are the individuals you should invest the most time and energy in training with competition in mind. They are the horses with the most potential to become the future stars of the turf or show ring.

Once the horses with the most potential according to your intended goals are identified, you need to establish training protocols that enable them to perform at peak levels. Entire books have been written on the subject of how to train horses according to discipline, and there is much to be learned from authors who specialize in a particular equestrian sport. But in this chapter I would like to highlight some of the keys of the Thomas Herding Technique that are important in training the Communicated Equine, and training him well, whatever his "job" or athletic pursuit.

The THT AirWorks System™

Among the most overlooked and underutilized aspects of sport horses is the reality that understanding and *training* the horse has to be approached on two fronts: you develop the athlete, you nurture the horse. No true training program is complete without knowing that physical conditioning allows the horse to cover distance, while mental conditioning allows the horse to control space. Learned experience and layering is an ongoing process in the cultivation of an athlete well prepared to perform.

The method I use to train the Communicated Equine is called the *THT Air-Works System.* Training any athlete for success means identifying and nurturing the *Emergent Properties* within the individual (see p. 3). The THT AirWorks System is designed to accomplish this by implementing training programs that develop and strengthen the mind, as well as the body, of the horse. There are several facets of the THT AirWorks System that should be applied to all serious horse training regimens.

Establish a Playbook of Training Protocols

In the wild, with the ability to roam and run free, horses learn how to discover their hidden, inner potential in the natural way. They learn how to run fast and, when necessary, become good jumpers. They learn how to escape the deathly claws of the mountain lion and sharp fangs of the wolf pack. But in the domestic environment, where horses are often confined to stalls day in and day out, there is no such means of self-discovery. Therefore, like the coach on the basketball court or football field, it is your job as rider, handler, and trainer to develop a *playbook,* a training strategy, and *coach* the horses in your stable in their journey to excelling in any manner of disciplines (figs. 8.1 A & B).

Work with Both the Basic and the Acquired Instinct

When training a horse for any discipline, you are simply progressively *assimilating* the horse to new tasks and experiences. Like his cousins in the wild, the domestic horse assimilates remarkably well because of his natural ability to survive by reacting consistently to certain stimuli or triggers of behavior. Training a horse is the art of *nurturing that which is natural* by gently nudging the horse along in one direction or another. Nature and horse do the rest for you.

To be effective at training the horse, you must never forget that the *basic instinct* and *acquired instinct* have a lot of influence on the behavior of the horse (see p. 15). Basic instinct can never be removed or altered entirely as it represents the horse's survival mechanism. Acquired instinct is molded by numerous environmental factors that include life in the herd, interactions with other animals on the farm, and associations with the humans in the horse's life. Both good and bad behaviors have their roots in the *acquired instinct* and that instinct is greatly influenced by the human presence in the Equine Circle.

8.1 A & B Training cross-country through different environments is extremely healthy and should be part of your playbook (training strategy). Physically your horse goes up and down hills over various terrains. Mentally, you give your horse natural environmental stimuli to interpret (A).

Traveling in and out of shadows helps horses become more comfortable with surface transitions and identifying things at their feet (B).

Create a Natural Training Environment

Creating and/or using the proper training environment in which to coach your equine athlete is of vital importance. The environment impacts learning ability because how information is *delivered* governs how that information is *received.* The biggest barrier for success in training the horse is that most equine athletic training programs do not take into account the influence of the environment or the Natural Herd Dynamic (see p. 99). I like to incorporate work beyond the track or practice ring, with lots of time cross-country and outside fenced-in areas. A horse presented with natural stimuli, such as undulations in footing and changing light (shadows and sun glare), while in motion, layers new memories over old. All learning and mental growth happens within the interpretation of stimuli and layered experiences. This is also where you tap into the naturally occurring inclination to target and anticipate, which when nurtured and honed, is key to developing top equine athletes.

Targeted Training of the Equine Athlete

Through research and the development of the Thomas Herding Technique, I have assigned the following areas for targeted training in equine athletes:

- Mental stimulus training designed to elevate the horse to a higher level by learning to rely less on the communication dialect of *body language* and more on the communication dialect of *intent* (p. 109).

- Mental stimulus training designed to train the mind to control and influence the body. *Patterns of behavior equal patterns of motion,* and it is important to develop proper patterns of behavior in order for the horse to perform at peak levels (p. 112).

- Time-in-motion training designed to teach the *emotional horse* to maintain Focus Agility and pace during periods of prolonged time-in-motion (p. 114).

- Time-in-motion training designed to help the *physical horse* develop stamina (air work) during periods of prolonged time-in-motion (p. 119).

Communication-of-Intent Training

Physical genetics breeds the horse, behavioral genetics produces the athlete. Nature's design for the horse is to be physically and mentally fit in order to ensure survival of the herd, and as I've said before, it is important for us as caretakers of the horse to implement nature's design into our training and breeding program. The most important aspect of training you will ever implement is the nurturing of your horse's mind.

It is far easier to *train for physical fitness* than it is to *nurture mental ability.* Nurturing the Emotional Conformation of the horse means operating within his communication dynamic as a *translator of intent.* The essence of Communication-of-Intent Training is to *train the horse to anticipate motion or movement before the physical act is accomplished* (fig. 8.2). Communication is inherently important because it allows the horse to learn, to grow, to move forward, to face challenges. Your own ability to cultivate communication of intent in your horse rests squarely on your depth of understanding of the communication dynamics in the herd (see p. 92).

8.2 Communication-of-Intent Training teaches the horse to anticipate motion or movement before the physical act is accomplished—a skill that could elevate the mediocre cutting horse to a top money-earner.

Natural Lead Position

In the wild, the natural inclination of a lead horse is to lead the herd from anywhere he deems necessary in order to accomplish his goal—the front, the side, or rear of the herd. This can affect a horse's performance, depending on the sport. For example, in a steeplechase or flat race, high-level horses might be inclined to lead "their" herd from a particular place in the field, so it is important to implement training programs that will coach them to always lead from the *front*.

Avoid "Melt-Aways"

You don't want your horse, while running in a race, to react to stimuli—other horses, track conditions, crowd noises—in a way that will compromise his speed and pace, and likewise, you don't want the ability of a dressage horse to transition smoothly from movement to movement to be sacrificed because of distraction (figs. 8.3 A & B). Like the lead horse in the wild, if for some reason your high-end equine athlete feels "threatened" during a competition, for reasons of survival, he will seek safety and withdraw, from communication with his rider and from the source of the perceived threat—think of a horse "melting away" from the lead on the racetrack or a dressage horse "checking out" after spooking in one corner of the arena. This is why it is so vitally important to nurture mental fitness in high-end horses—they

8.3 A & B Allowing race-horses to battle for space during workouts is a good mental preparedness tool in order to prevent the horse reacting poorly to stimuli during competition. Here, the horse on the inside is showing great concentration as he looks to take the space away from the horse on the outside (A).

Schooling dressage horses in a variety of settings, including group and solo clinic situations, both crowded and empty practice rings, goes a long way toward nurturing the horse's ability to "multitask"—to focus on his work despite multiple stimuli (B).

8.4 Training horses in groups, creating a herd environment in which to work them, is beneficial for the emotional preparedness of the equine athlete. Whenever possible, three or more horse should be ridden together. This applies particularly to the racehorse, as racing conditions can be recreated, but is also of value in terms of Communication-of-Intent and Patterns-of-Motion Training for other sports.

must have a strong sense of anticipation of what's ahead of them, allowing them to take the lead and stay in the lead because their intent is to *influence what is "just around the bend."*

Be it a racehorse, dressage horse, or any equine athlete for that matter, *efficiency of motion* is in the horse's ability to transition properly. This ability to transition while in motion is nurtured within the communication dynamics of the horse. You will advance further, and more consistently, the horse that is able to identify and, at the highest levels, *anticipate* intent—of other horses, of humans, of livestock. Without that training, the horse will frequently perform in an inconsistent manner. But this requires you properly nurture the mind of the Communicated Equine—*the highest levels of horsemanship lie within the translation of intent rather than the interpretation of body language.*

Communication-of-Intent Training—
Sample Mental Stimulus Exercise

When your goal is to improve a horse's ability to *anticipate intent,* you are actually aiming to improve his ability to *communicate.* This can be done by working the horse in close proximity with one other horse, or several others—for example, galloping in a group on the track, using a lead horse while schooling cross-country obstacles, and working on 10- and 20-meter circles at the same time and in the same space as another horse and rider (fig. 8.4). This kind of "close-contact" exercise helps your horse learn to anticipate moves before they happen and is useful for all breeds and disciplines.

Patterns-of-Behavior Training

Physical training of the horse is important, but, training only for that is training for mediocrity. *Real* athletic training means the act of training the mind to control and influence the body. The difference in one's achievement in the show ring or on the racetrack often comes in the gray area that lies between changing the focus from pure, physical training to that of mental training in order to advance to the next level.

Understanding how singular pieces of the horse psyche fit together and how those pieces communicate the outer world to the horse allows you to begin to identify patterns of behavioral genetics. Patterns within the horse's behavior directly influence his individual patterns of motion; therefore, the way a horse moves tells you a lot about his behavior, and vice versa.

8.5 Some insecure horses seek comfort while travelling in a herd and just want to run next to another horse. Even if they have the physical ability to win the race, they will stick with a buddy or wait for slower horses, instead of releasing and thinking forward.

To illustrate, let's take the sport of flat racing. If you watch any horse race and closely observe the participants, a pattern of motion can be identified for each horse. Some horses like close contact, some control the space of other horses from the front or just off their flank, some are controlled by other horses, while others wait and appear content to "buddy-up" with another for the duration of their time-in-motion.

What do these patterns of motion indicate? The combative horse likes the challenge of competition and seeks to control the space of another horse. This is especially true of high-level horses that often seem to offer a challenge for the pure gamesmanship of defeating another horse. On the other end of the spectrum, the horse that will "buddy-up" and run neck and neck with another horse during a race can have issues of insecurity and needs to run with a comfortable companion to feel safe in motion (fig. 8.5). Any number of different aberrations and anomalies can influence the efficiency of motion of the athlete. The horse's ability to communicate and even anticipate is often the deciding factor of where he is located within the herd in motion.

The THT AirWorks system is a powerful training tool that can help horses change poor behavioral patterns and patterns of motion. The insecure horse can be taught with Mental Stimulus Exercises and Patterns-of-Behavior Training to be a better interpreter of environmental stimuli and the *intentions* of other horses when the herd is in motion. The high-spirited horse that likes to challenge other horses can be taught to "catch and release" an opponent in order to move forward toward other targets, such as the finish line of a race.

Patterns-of-Behavior Training—Sample Mental Stimulus Exercise

I once worked with a polo pony who was highly skilled athletically but unable to transition from one target to the next—from one competing horse-and-rider team to another, for example—an important skill in the fast-action sport of polo. I prescribed a patterns-of-motion exercise in which we asked the horse to manage multiple stimuli all around him, while in motion, while maintaining focus on *only one* target. The goal was to teach him that he should focus on whatever his rider wanted him to focus on—in this case, just the one target, be it ball, goal, or competing team member. Next we added a quick turn from the rider and a second, new target to focus on. This exercise ultimately improved the horse's ability to make quick and efficient transitions.

Time-in-Motion: Focus and Pace Training

As we've discussed, Focus Agility is the natural ability of the horse to interpret stimulus while in motion. The ability to maintain *pace over distance and time-in-motion* is determined by the mental capacity or Focus Agility within the Emotional Conformation of the horse. This synergy allows the horse to accelerate or decelerate without injury. For example, *physical ability* in certain sport horses, such as the Thoroughbred, is often measured by the speed over which a distance of ground is covered, whereas *mental ability* is measured by the *pace of the time-in-motion.* Pace is determined by the mental ability to focus over a given space of time, speed is determined by the physical ability within that given space—motion thus becomes the collateral effect of the two combined.

A true understanding of how the horse views time-in-motion begins with a simple equation: *time of activity is relative to time of inactivity.* Thus, pace and speed accelerate or decelerate in relative unison. Mental conditioning, therefore, must supersede physical ability in order to maintain both pace and accelerated levels of motion (speed) in smooth transitions. This is because the time afforded the horse to interpret stimuli is diminished relative to the speed at which the horse is moving.

Maximizing Focus Agility

If I want my horse to run a mile, I train him to be as physically fit as possible in order to successfully achieve that goal. However, this does not allow for training of pace. To train for pace, the horse must be properly prepared, mentally, to maintain Focus Agility over a sustained period of time-in-motion. In order to maximize Focus Agility, if the horse needs to be in motion for two minutes of competition, the horse should be trained to maintain focus for four minutes—and so on.

Motion should not be confused with *speed*—it is not trained for or elevated in the same manner. Training for physical speed by getting the horse physically fit to cover a distance of ground is obviously necessary in some sports. Covering that distance efficiently and with pace requires the horse to negotiate his time-in-motion. The ability to stay focused while moving ultimately determines the time at which the distance will be covered.

A Human Exercise in Understanding Focus Agility and Time-in-Motion

A good experiment to measure Focus Agility and how it affects time-in-motion is to visit a running track and time how long it takes you to walk a lap on several consecutive days. The first day of this experiment perhaps you make an effort to concentrate on your motion. Smooth and relaxed in your walk, never losing focus, you cross the line and click your stopwatch. The next day you repeat the exercise, but maybe this time you are not so mentally focused because there are other people walking or running laps. Distracted by them, your mind wanders a bit. Although you are the *same athlete* covering the *same distance,* your time is slower because of the distraction. You can easily see how concentration while in motion and sur-rounded by multiple stimuli (Focus Agility) determines how *time-in-motion* and *distance* are anything but the same. Try repeating the exercise over the course of a couple of weeks, and practice managing the stimuli you perceive during your walks with the intention of regulating your end time—in essence, improving your own Focus Agility.

Reeling-In Focus

It is also important to note the relevancy of time-in-motion and Focus Agility when you consider the number of precise movements an equine athlete such as a dressage or reining horse performs over a prolonged period of time (figs. 8.6 A & B). A great deal of focus and mental aptitude, as well as physical stamina, is

8.6 A & B Dressage and reining horses are expected to perform a series of pre-cise movements seamlessly, at varying speeds, and over a prolonged period of time. This requires enhanced Focus Agility on the part of these equine athletes in or-der to maintain self-control despite multiple stimuli.

required to perform exacting tasks, sometimes in rapid succession. Eliminating "knee-jerk" reactions to variable stimuli is vital to horses who need strong self-control and internal focus, such as the dressage and reining horse.

For this type of nurturing and coaching, the horse's mental focus must be *targeted far away* and then *reeled in.* In other words, you want to develop a program that requires your horse maintain his focus while managing stimuli at a distance. One way to do this is to present a target far in front of your horse, have it gradually close in on the horse ("reel it in"), and then allow the horse to eventually pass it. This builds and strengthens the horse's Focus Agility as you continue to bring the stimuli closer and closer, elevating the demands of the horse to *hold form and position* even with a complexity of challenges moving toward him. Along this path your horse's strengths and *behavioral overcompensations*—adjustments on the part of the horse, due to a perceived sense restriction, that have a negative effect on the horse's pattern of motion (see p. 141)—will be revealed, allowing you to further hone the training system you are designing for your equine athlete.

For the horse to be trained in such a way that will allow for a natural (and efficient) flow of movement, you must understand that time-in-motion is the only

Kerry's Corner

Question: **Seeing your depth of thought on the subject of the horse, what are the psychological differences from setting a pace and training for or obtaining a certain speed?**
—Mr. Weld, European Thoroughbred Industry

Answer: I will start by stating my personal mantra from which my work in the area of equine mental agility and focus stems: *Pace is determined by the mental ability to focus over a given space of time; speed is determined by the physical ability to react within that given space; motion thus becomes the collateral effect of the two combined.*

Think of it this way: consider a bullet from a gun as compared to a long-distance runner. The bullet has *speed,* but it cannot have *pace,* for it is dependent solely on the device from which it erupted for its *time-in-motion.* The long-distance runner can have *both* speed and pace, which is based upon *mental recognition* of both the *motion itself* and the *stimuli affecting it.* The runner's time-in-motion, then, is reflective of his speed controlled by the pace, which can go up *or* down, at any time. The bullet, only having speed, is moving as fast as it ever will at the eruption of motion and slowing down ever after because it has no pace to control or influence that speed.

The Thoroughbred racehorse is a runner, not a bullet. Therefore, knowing the ability to focus manifested in the Herd Dynamic level naturally occurring in the horse, as well as the horse's inclination to "move up," will assist you a great deal both in understanding your equine athlete's natural ability and potential level in training, in addition to the development of training protocols.

measure needed. The horse's Emergent Properties (and mental capacity) ultimately allow him to safely and quickly identify the rapid influx of stimuli experienced as speed and complexity of performance challenges (longer distances, higher fences, more collection) increases.

Speed Extended in Time

Famed Thoroughbred breeder Federico Tesio was also one of the great trainers of all time, and in *Breeding the Racehorse* he noted the importance of speed in a sporting event: "From the atom to the star, the life of the universe is based on speed extended in time. Among living beings, speed extended in time means staying power."

Mental stimulus training protocols can be developed as part of the overall process to elevate the individual equine athlete by using this simple equation: *physical* energy (speed) plus *emotional* energy (ability to focus and maintain pace) equals *time-in-motion*. For the horse, speed is relative to circumstance, which is governed by *perceived need* or *environmental influences*. The horse's interpretation of environmental stimuli and your use of it as a training tool is a key to balancing the mind and body, making your horse more efficient in his performance. *Physical efficiency*

It isn't always the *speedy horse* you seek but rather the horse with a high degree of focus. This is determined in the Emotional Conformation Profile of your horse with the P-Type grade used as a guide (see p. 78). It is important to note that Focus Agility and steady or elevated pace can be trained in association with time-in-motion. This means that you can nurture the inherent mental capacity to elevated levels with perceived stimuli. This stems from the concept of *association,* or for the horse, *triggers* by way of association.

Developing triggers that work by way of association works in a similar manner with humans. For example, I could not remember the code for my keyless entry. The numbers were 3-3-9-5-7, but I just always drew a blank until I *associated* them with the ketchup name "33 Heinz 57." To this day I have *never* forgotten this association. You can use variable types of similar stimuli in association to gain your intended result on a consistent basis with your horse, and in time, this develops what might appear to be *anticipation*.

Speed being the byproduct of pace in an athlete, human or equine, true training must first embrace the expansion of mental capacity and focus ability while in motion—so the human or horse doesn't *lose pace* with the influx of stimuli. The athlete having the ability to focus for an extended period of time-in-motion is the key to success. If you nurture the mind and allow the body to evolve to its needed strength for the horse's intended sport, when you begin your *real training* for competition, your horse will have a serious head start over others.

translates into speed and staying power. *Mental efficiency* rests within the horse's ability to communicate and translate an influx of environmental stimuli.

Teach the horse to focus, and you coach the horse to achieve. The goal is to help equine athletes find ways to *become more efficient*—both in movement and in decision-making while in motion. Indeed, properly training the equine athlete on an emotional level will unlock the totality of his awesome physical powers and cultivate his inclination to become a natural leader and champion, in the show ring or on the racetrack.

Time-in-Motion—Focus and Pace Sample Exercise

When your horse is expected to perform in competition for a period of two to five minutes, regardless of the discipline, your horse should be able to move at a steady pace for much longer than that (at least 10 or 20 minutes). To improve your horse's ability to focus and pace himself in competition, work him in company at a steady pace over extended periods of time. You can do this at a jog or trot, or even a walk. The key is to maintain an even speed for an extended period of time—depending on the gait, probably a distance of 3 to 5 miles. As I will discuss in stamina-building

Kerry's Corner

Question: **I have been searching for a long time a way to better understand the concept of distance and how the horse "comprehends" his own pace. I am seeking ways to devise better training tools for my horses that will allow me to introduce a more natural flow to distance and also assist my jockeys' strategy. Can you shed a little light on this subject so we as trainers can maybe evolve the ways in which we breeze our horses?**
—Thoroughbred Trainer, United States

Answer: When it comes to the ways in which we as *humans* see distance and the ways *the horse* sees or comprehends distance, our two observations are very different. When we humans run a race, we know we have a Point A and a Point B, and we work to cover the distance between them in as short as time as possible. When a horse is put into the same situation, as in a race, the horse simply acts upon natural instincts (that we encourage)—that is to gallop and to do it more efficiently or faster than the next horse. The actual *distance* the horse covers is measured only by the length of time the horse is asked to move. We humans may look at an object that is 100 meters away and use it as our objective marker; the horse moves more or less in open space, without markers. For the horse, the only difference between 5 furlongs and 8 is the time he spends in motion, and even this is of little interest to the horse—he is on the move only as long as his interpretation of stimuli is asking for this motion.

(see below), you want to mentally condition your horse *far beyond* what he needs to do during competition, whether it is a dressage test, a reining pattern, a hunter course, or a race.

Time-in-Motion: Training for Stamina

Fatigue is the number one enemy of the equine athlete. When horses get tired, they lose their ability to maintain both focus and pace. However, time-in-motion training inherent in the THT AirWorks System comes with a positive side-affect— physical endurance. It is my core belief that properly coaching or training equine athletes actually requires *overtraining* them on both the physical and mental level. Not in a foolish, unhealthy way, of course, but within the confines of their ability. Quite simply, horses should be physically and mentally prepared to accomplish *far more* than what will be required of them in a given event.

To train horses to maintain focus and build stamina, too, you must train *way over* your conditioning goals, and then gradually work inward, shrinking the distance covered or time under saddle while increasing speed or difficulty of move-

The most difficult thing for humans to imagine is infinity; we gear our lives in such a way that we build "boxes" to neatly fit around our various worlds. We are encased with starting points and ending points. The closest thing we come to naturally understanding how a horse envisions time and space is by the watch or clock that tells us we may be late if that driver in front of us doesn't get going. For the horse to be trained in such a way that will allow a *natural flow of movement,* we must understand that it is *time-in-motion* that is the only measuring stick we need heed. This lends itself to the streamlining of efficiency, which can be implemented by two things: the ability of the mind to focus on the stimuli that cause the motion, and the environmental stimuli that influence the motion. That is to say, it is the *senses* and the *interpretation of the Herd Dynamic* (see p. 99) that dictate the pace and the time of any motion. A horse reacts to a blowing sagebrush with a quick turn. The same horse reacts to an approaching predator by moving quickly away for a longer period of time—the horse is seeking not more *distance* between he and the stimuli, but more *space.* It is important to understand that for the horse a "predator" is any perceived stimulus that evokes a sense of danger. His interpretation of, and therefore your use of stimuli, both as the cause of motion and the environmental influences that dictate time and direction, are the keys to balancing the horse's mind and body, thus making him more *efficient* on the hoof. Efficiency then translates into speed and staying power.

ment, as well as the horse's mental conditioning, to make smooth transitions during an escalated time-in-motion.

Time-in-Motion—Stamina Sample Exercise

A racehorse with a P-Type grade for distance aptitude (see p. 82) should be first worked at gallops and trots of 3 to 4 miles with a balanced seat rider sitting down on his back. Then, once speed and pace work begins, the long workouts can be cut back to 1½ to 2 miles at the maximum.

An endurance prospect also needs to have daily workouts over distance and multiple types of terrain. Stamina work should be performed at varying speeds while asking the horse to deal with multiple stimuli over protracted periods of time. *Interval training*—"slow" at first, from a mental training viewpoint (that is, working great distances at a jog, without adding much in the way of mental stimuli), then moving the speed up in stages, ideally at different elevations, and adding multiple stimuli—is extremely useful. Only horses with the highest level Herd Dynamic (see p. 99) are able to succeed at the top levels of endurance racing.

Confidence and Reaction Time

Confidence is one of the most important qualities that equine athletes need, and the THT AirWorks training program I've outlined here, focusing on patterns of motion and time-in-motion, is designed to build confidence in the horse. The horse who is self-reliant, who is able to negotiate and interpret variable stimuli without a physical reaction, will ultimately have the ability to perform at the highest level.

Confidence and decision-making in the horse is dependent on environmental and associated trigger stimuli—they are governing factors for action. Swiftness of action or reaction is determined by smooth translation of information by the horse. Once the *mind* gives the succinct and confident order to move, the body reacts, and the time between these two actions is the *latent space*. This space or time of *latency* is the measure of the horse's confidence, and in effect, it governs the ability of the horse to focus—which we've already identified as being crucial during a race or sporting event.

The latent space between interpretation and action or non-action is hardly, if ever, perceptible. However, the horse who has a more prolonged space between interpretation and action or non-action is the horse who lacks confidence and may be more dependent on the herd for direction. This horse is not "free" or self-assured

8.7 A–E This is a basic example of a THT AirWorks patterns-of-motion exercise in action. I am working with two Thoroughbred-Oldenburg crosses—both dressage horses—Sophie (lead horse) and Shane (rear) at the Pine Knoll Center for Integrated Horsemanship in Lexington, Kentucky.

By keeping the lead horse straight and the rear horse moving in an S-pattern close behind, we are asking the front horse to travel toward a target (me) while identifying moving stimulus behind her in multiple vision planes. This technique can be utilized in many different drills, regardless of speed (gait).

Alternating fields of view can simulate multiple horses behind, or create the effect of other potential distractions. The lead horse must repeatedly target and release what is behind, while maintaining efficient forward motion.

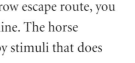

enough to manage the interpretation of stimuli that is required to maintain the prolonged focus necessary in demanding sporting events, such as upper level eventing and dressage.

In the wild, the development of confidence occurs naturally. That is nature's way of selecting the most mentally capable horse to be the leader. On the move, the herd is dependent upon the most confident, focused horse to lead during times of high stress. For example, if you watch a herd of wild horses running from danger and being forced to funnel into a narrow escape route, you may well see the hierarchy defined as they file into a single line. The horse who is emotionally sound and confident is not distracted by stimuli that does not affect his well-being, and his probability of success is greatly increased. In the case of the racehorse, the weight of the jockey on his back, the roar of the crowd, the pent-up, explosive energy of the other horses in the starting gate are all factors potentially interfering with his ability to focus. The horse who smoothly processes all this information is the horse who wins the race (figs. 8.7 A–E).

Thoughts on Training According to Age and Maturation

Yearlings

Training the yearling is a highly sensitive time as acquired instinct (see p. 16) is rapidly developing, making the introduction of new information that requires serious concentration often overwhelming and confusing for the horse. When the horse is confused, a trigger (see p. 19) may be activated and negative behavior may result. Therefore, during this time it is important not to "overload" the young horse. Short bursts of information, daily, with extremely attentive handling and communication are paramount. Otherwise, the flight response might be engaged with every incoming stimulus.

In order to flee from danger and therefore survive in the wild, the horse had to evolve as an animal that associates with immediate environmental stimuli. Immediate stimulus association and layered learning are the guiding lights of the acquired instinct, creating a mentally active and emotional horse. Consequently, positive triggers are very important and negative human interactions with the horse should be avoided at all costs. The first year is a time when proper communication between horse and human is a most influential training tool.

Two-Year-Olds

Juvenile filly and colt training can be more intense than that used with yearlings, but care should still be taken not to overload the young horse with too much information. Remember, you are often asking the horse to do things that are in opposition to his very nature. Most of the Individual Horse Personality is complete by now, making it easier to observe, by virtue of your horse's quirks, negative behavior or stress issues. It is important to note that your horse can be retrained (reconditioned), and as noted earlier in this chapter possesses an evolved associative learning dynamic that works in synchronicity with an associative memory dynamic—all governed, of course, by the basic instinct (see p. 15). An immediate positive reward or experience will link associative learning to an associative memory—a trigger—and you want that memory to be positive, not negative. It is important to make the environment for your young horse as comfortable as possible, as comfort for the horse is reward. Unlike in the wild, if your horse is uncomfortable with his domestic environment he cannot leave it to go elsewhere. This inability of your horse to flee to safety and comfort can manifest in the form of stress or bad behavior at this age.

The horse is not "forward-thinking" and does not reason the results of his behavior, but reacts instinctively in either a basic or acquired manner. Therefore, uncovering, and then handling, behavior issues requires an Emotional Conformation Profile of your horse's Individual Horse Personality, as well as an assessment of your horse's fears. *Fear assessment* through a process I use called *reverse association* (a means of identifying associative memories that formed triggers of negative behavior) can work to resocialize your horse to his current environment through the use of Assimilated Imprinting of positive stimuli that result in positive behavior.

Older Horses

Older horses have deep-rooted memory associations that can become habitual comfort zones for everyday behavior. That behavior can be either good or bad, and with so much more associative memory in place, there is less and less "room" for Assimilated Imprinting of your horse. However, new associative learning and socialization behavior training can occur once you understand the horse's Emotional Conformation and the makeup of his acquired instinct.

Knowing this information about your horse's psyche is useful for socializing the horse into new herds or new environments. *Socialization training* is the act of introducing a horse, young or old, in slow increments, to new environmental stimuli. It is impossible to have a long-lasting influence on your horse and reconfigure his acquired instinct without first studying the dynamics of its creation.

Benefits of the THT AirWorks System

Horses in the wild discover their potential in the natural way. The THT AirWorks System incorporates all the elements of the Natural Herd Dynamic in a training program designed to help domestic horses discover their deep, hidden, inner potential so they can become the future stars of equine sport (fig. 8.8). By Mother Nature's design, horses learn best while in motion, and the decisions they make "on the hoof" have the most impact on self-preservation. The AirWorks system utilizes

8.8 The THT AirWorks System incorporates all the elements of the Natural Herd Dynamic—learning in motion, learning via communication, and learning via the rules of natural selection—in a training program designed to help domestic horses discover their deep, hidden, inner potential so they can become the future stars of the turf or the show ring.

the ability of the horse to learn on the move and incorporates that Natural Herd Dynamic in a mental stimulus training program designed to enhance the focus and physical ability of the equine athlete to perform at peak levels, whatever his age, whatever his specialty. Conscientious focus on the targeted areas described in this chapter, when well informed regarding your horse's Emotional Conformation, can also help prevent development of *Potential Withholds* and *Equine Mental Illness,* which I talk about next.

9 The Broken Circle: Potential Withholds and Equine Mental Illness

"Being so adaptable and compliant is the precipice from which the horse can fall into behavioral aberrations."

Once you enter the Equine Circle and take the steps necessary to form a playbook of training protocols for your horse, you may discover that your horse or others in your stable have "issues" affecting their quality of farm life or performance on the racetrack or in the show ring. Performance is not always indicative of actual ability; a poor performance can be due to behavioral problems. Often, the root cause of those problems is a direct result of living in the domestic environment, which we outlined in chapter 3 (p. 27).

In the wild, the horse is free to roam and graze. However, in the domestic environment, the world of the Equine Circle is restricted by a life spent mostly in stalls and in training. Unlike his cousins in the wild, the horse in the domestic environment is completely dependent on man for his survival and well-being. As mentioned, the way a horse is handled, who or what he is exposed to, indeed, every aspect of the controlled equine world containing our human element is the environment our horse perceives and experiences. The environment is the foundation of life experience for the horse, and it is often the trigger of unseen stress and behavior issues we only observe much later as the horse grows older and starts in a training program. When horses develop behavioral problems, the Equine Circle is broken.

Potential Withholds and Equine Mental Illness

Two sources of behavioral problems are what I call *Potential Withholds*—anything of a physical, but mostly mental, nature that restricts the horse and prevents him from living up to his fullest potential—and *Equine Mental Illness,* which is best described as any mental distress or psychosis (worst case) that impedes the horse's performance and overall quality of life.

An investigation of the environmental influences and the psyche of your horse can often reveal the Potential Withholds preventing him from attaining his potential. If not properly dealt with, stress the horse endures in training to become a top, world-class athlete can lead to Equine Mental Illness. In most cases, such disorders are only revealed by the horse's poor performance. Does your racehorse have the natural physical ability to beat the field and be a winner but comes in second, third, or last in most of his races? Is this the result of the track condition, the jockey, the trainer, or an emotional Potential Withhold? Does your event horse go clean and fast over cross-country only to pull rails in show jumping? Is this because of poor conditioning, poor riding, or something else?

If you believe your horse has the potential to be a good performer but always seems stuck at a certain level when competing, then your horse could have Potential Withholds affecting his performance, as well as his ability to interact with other horses.

The Eight Key Causes of Behavioral Problems

Equine Mental Illness and Potential Withholds can be tremendous barriers, preventing the horse from living up to his fullest potential. In my years of study of this subject, I have identified eight key causes of behavioral problems that can affect the quality of farm life, and ultimately, the performance of the horse.

- Weaning: Removing the young horse too soon from the family structure can become a Potential Withhold that has lifelong consequences resulting in poor performance for the equine athlete (p. 127).

- Stress: Hidden stresses the horse suffers as he adapts to the environmental and social changes of life are powerful Potential Withholds (p. 130).

- Behavior Triggers: Triggers from the acquired instinct and associative memories of the horse can be a major Potential Withhold for the horse—and especially for the equine athlete (p. 135).

- Handling and Training Protocols: These can be a source of Potential Withholds if they are used to force the horse to do something he is not physically or mentally capable of achieving (p. 139).

- Behavioral Overcompensation: This can be a disastrous Potential Withhold, causing the racehorse to alter his running style or the show horse to falter in competition (p. 141).

- Equine Cabin Fever: Confinement in stalls, especially for the convalescing horse, can be a devastating Potential Withhold, with prolonged confinement possibly resulting in Equine Mental Illness (p. 145).

- Human Attachment Disorder: This is a horrendous behavioral disorder for the horse who develops attachments to owners and handlers and is then sold to another stable. It can be especially devastating for retired equine athletes. Untreated, Human Attachment Disorder can result in mental illness (p. 148).

- Equine Abandonment Syndrome: All horses can experience this syndrome but it mostly occurs in equine athletes who, after several years of competition, feel a sudden sense of loss and abandonment when retired. Untreated, Equine Abandonment Syndrome can result in mental illness (p. 153).

Diagnosing behavioral problems can sometimes be difficult, as many of the problems have the same symptoms. It also is not uncommon for horses to suffer from several behavioral disorders. For example, stress and behavioral overcompensations can, but not always, be a result of a behavior trigger from a previous life experience. Acting up in the paddock or warm-up ring and balking at entering the starting gate or show pen can stem from the horse being excited and agitated by the noise of the crowd, or it could be the result of a behavior trigger.

Finding the root cause of a behavior disorder or disorders can be difficult and time consuming. Throughout the rest of this chapter, we will look at the eight key causes of behavioral problems and several case studies outlining related conditions. (Unless noted, the names of the horses and owners in the stories ahead have been changed to ensure confidentiality and privacy.)

Weaning

One of the most traumatic events that can result in Potential Withholds for the young horse is when he is taken from a structured family unit far too early. How we do not understand this as fact for the socially dependent horse when examples abound in our own species boggles the mind. Imagine being taken from your parents when you were extremely young, and being moved to a strange new home where you are one of several children and young adults from various backgrounds. Even if the new home is filled with love and kindness, there will still be "something" missing—and it is this that can become a source of severe emotional and behavioral problems in the horse (fig. 9.1).

And so it often is with weanlings: they are taken from their family-oriented, social environment and thrust into a group of other "lost" young horses. Usually, a handler or trainer asks these youngsters to do things they have never done before, which combined with the stress of weaning from their dam, can be a cause of Potential Withholds that affects their overall development. These withholds can have a lasting effect and later impact the horse when he is old enough to race or show. We don't push our own children out the door until they are mature enough to handle themselves in certain situations, so why do we have such different expectations when it comes to young horses?

I have found that young horses, especially colts, who are cut from the family herd far too early have a multitude of bridges to cross when they start athletic training—none of them easy. Over the years, I've see a lot of horses who suffer from these—what I call "weaning scars"—which are due to a factory-like, corporate approach to weaning. As seen in the wild, the longer a young horse has to mature

9.1 The connection between mare and young foal is vital. Weaning too soon can cause behavioral problems with lifelong consequences, including poor performance in the equine athlete.

within his family unit, the better off he will ultimately be. When raised in a herd environment, the young horse learns how to identify the movements and intentions of other horses—this is crucial if the horse is to embark on a career as an equine athlete. The young horse also learns how to recognize his own Emergent Properties (see p. 1) and inner potential through interaction with other horses in the herd. The young horse that is "socially sound" has a trainable mind—he will learn faster and be a better achiever, which is of primary importance in the competitive sport horse.

When weaning, a gradual transition from a young horse's family to his new "herd" is best, and even after weaning, he should remain stabled and pastured with older horses, both before and after training begins. This is a critical time of mental growth for the young horse as he learns from the older horses many of the important communication skills necessary for equine survival—important even in the artificial, domesticated environment (see p. 27). The skills the young horse learns living in the herd will prove to be invaluable when he finally enters formal training.

CASE STUDY

Butch: The Erratic Racehorse

The Problem

One day, a client named Susan called to see if I could help improve the performance of Butch—a Thoroughbred racehorse she had recently claimed. Susan explained that Butch was four years old. He had been racing since he was two and always seemed to train well, but his performance on the racetrack was erratic and inconsistent. Butch would act up in the paddock and at the starting gate. He seemed hesitant and appeared confused before a race. During a race, Butch was protective of his space and content to "buddy-up" and run with another horse.

I agreed to help and asked Susan to send some film footage of Butch's previous races. After viewing five of his races and taking into account the above characteristics, it was clear to me that Butch suffered from a Potential Withhold that afflicts a lot of equine athletes—he had been weaned too early.

The Solution

The "therapy" I prescribed for Butch required him to be placed in a training program where he could learn many of the basic skills that he did not learn when he was weaned too early. All horses, be they wild or domestic, learn best when in motion, so I created a patterns-of-motion "playbook" for Susan to use in training Butch. The playbook is a tool of the THT AirWorks System (see chapter 8, p. 105), which is designed to train sport horses and release their inner potential so they can perform better. Learning how to communicate and interact with other horses, knowing how to understand and anticipate their intentions when the herd was at rest or in motion, were vital skills that Butch would need to learn if he was going to advance beyond the claiming ranks to higher levels of racing competition.

To teach Butch the basics of herd communication and interaction, a series of patterns-of-motion exercises on the racetrack were developed. Butch was worked in company with an older, seasoned mare—she was a skillful mover, and the goal of the exercise was to teach Butch how to understand and anticipate the intentions or intended motion of the mare as the pair moved over the training track. Initially, we had Butch follow in the footsteps of the mare, about one length behind. As the training progressed the distance between the pair was extended to two lengths and then finally three. The purpose of extending the gap between the two was to strengthen Butch's *Focus Agility,* which is a skill young horses learn through daily interaction with the herd. Focus Agility is crucial for the competitive equine athlete—think of the cutting horse on a cow or the jumper approaching the final combination on course.

Another patterns-of-motion exercise required Butch to follow the mare as she zigzagged left to right and back in a snake-like pattern. This also helped to strengthen his Focus Agility, as well as reinforcing his ability to anticipate every movement of the mare. After the third day, Butch and the mare were working in perfect unison. When the mare moved right, Butch moved right. When the mare moved left, Butch moved left.

The next phase of the training required the pair to cover a distance of at least 5 miles at a much slower pace. This exercise was designed to strengthen Butch's ability to focus over a prolonged period of *time-in-motion* (physical energy plus emotional energy equals time-in-motion—see chapter 8, p. 114, for more about this), which is another crucial skill that a successful racehorse must possess. Finally, we taught Butch to target his workmate, catch her, and run beyond to take the lead. This exercise was designed to help Butch overcome his tendency to "buddy-up" with another horse during a race.

By the end of training, Butch no longer showed signs of hesitancy or confusion, and he moved with confidence over the training track. It appeared that the former claimer was ready to advance to the next racing level.

Stress

Stress with which the weanling struggles when cut from the herd too early is only the beginning of many stresses he will experience during his lifetime. Stress can be especially harmful for the horse, and often owners and handlers are not even aware that the horse is suffering from this problem. High-level horses will do their very best to hide stress and anxiety so they do not stand out from the rest of the herd. The horse's natural instinct is one of self-preservation, and the last thing he wants is to be noticed by a predator, which in some cases includes humans.

In fact, it is unlikely any of us ever truly see just how many times a day a form of stress and sudden change impacts our horse because it happens so quickly. It is not the stress we see that is always the most powerful, but the stress *we do not see*. In the tranquil pasture, even the most "quiet" horse can develop high levels of stress that go undetected. Then, when asked to participate in a training program, a race, a dressage competition, or even to simply go on a casual trail ride, the "quiet" horse in the pasture becomes a wild, unrideable beast.

The demands of training can have a profound effect on the horse and often become the source of stress and behavior issues. During high levels of activity, such as intense training, the basic instinct (see p. 15) controls 90 percent of what the horse perceives. In this high state of performance—whether during daily workouts, periods of increased levels of training, or competition—the basic instinct makes decisions based on pure reaction. Always edgy, ready to go, the horse's view of reality is not necessarily skewed, but it *is* accepted as truth. The horse has operated at such high levels with sustained environmental influences for so long, it quite simply becomes a way of life. The horse has been taught how to operate in, or in essence, *survive* his domestic environment. Over time, it may become evident that the horse seems jittery, and after years of intense training for competition, when asked to suddenly transition into a calmer career, the horse may well have serious adjustment issues. (Note that just because the "retired" equine athlete is placed in a relaxed and low-key environment doesn't mean he will automatically accept it or feel comfortable—to expect the horse to suddenly change and adapt to a brand new environment is unfounded, regardless of his age or state of competitive career.)

Confinement in stalls (see also Equine Cabin Fever, p. 145) is a powerful hindrance to the physical health and well-being of the horses in your stable, but it pales in comparison to the emotional problems horses can develop in a closed environment. Stress can be seen and then practically dealt with when it erupts in physical forms, such as bucking, biting, cribbing, and weaving. However, many of these issues are a physical manifestation of emotional problems. In such cases, socialization techniques need to be investigated and implemented during the time of adjustment to the new, indoor environment.

In order to minimize behavioral issues in the horse, nurturing the Natural Herd Dynamic in the domestic environment (see chapter 4, p. 35) goes a long way in help-

9.2 The demands of training and prolonged confinement in stalls can have a profound effect on the horse, resulting in stress and behavior issues. One method I use to measure and alleviate the stress level of the horse is a Breath Stress Test, where I create a rhythm of breathing with the horse to lower his stress level. I demonstrate this here with the pony Puzzle.

ing the horse to live a full, productive life, free from the mental hobbles of Potential Withholds and Equine Mental Illness. Breaking up the monotony of the mundane and "everyday" with *Mental Stimulus Exercises* is one of the best therapies for horses who spend most of their life confined in stalls. I also use what I call a *Breath Stress Test,* where I provide a breathing rhythm intended to "lead" the horse away from the source of his stress and to succumb to my calming influence (fig. 9.2).

CASE STUDY

Gritty Gal: The Racehorse Who Lost Her Grit
The Problem

The case of Gritty Gal is a perfect example of how environmental and social changes can lead to the development of stress in the horse. A change in environment can be a major source of stress for horses, especially when a gradual introduction to new surroundings is not available or practical.

Gritty Gal, a five-year-old Thoroughbred racehorse with a decent racing record, was purchased privately in the summer of 2002 as a prospective race mare. The new owner, who had hopes of racing Gritty Gal as a six-year-old, gave her several months off from the rigors of training and put her out in a lush pasture, along with several other horses, with the intention of allowing Gritty Gal to "just be a horse again."

Right from the start, Gritty Gal was unsettled in her new surroundings and appeared to be happiest when she was in her stall—she wouldn't associate with the other horses. Some horses readily adjust to change while others, like Gritty Gal, do not; in that respect, they aren't much different from humans. When faced with change, some of us look at it as an exciting adventure while others become moody and long for the way things used to be. Some may stubbornly resist change and even lash out at the forces pushing for it. Eventually, grudgingly or happily, we humans usually adjust, and such was the case with Gritty Gal. After several weeks on the farm she became so well adjusted she flourished, grazing in the lush meadows and pastures of her new environment. It soon became clear that Gritty Gal, the new kid on the block, had become the boss and dominant mare of the stable. The owner was happy to see the turnaround and looked forward to the day the mare would return to racing.

Finally training time rolled around. Every day the owner would load Gritty Gal into the trailer to take her to the nearby racetrack. Gritty Gal returned to her career as if she had never left—after all, she was a professional. She had great workouts, attracting a lot of attention from onlookers at the track.

However, as training progressed, loading Gritty Gal into the trailer became more difficult. She became stressed and washed out during the struggle to load her. The exercise rider noticed that she didn't seem to be on top of her game; she didn't stand out from the other horses like she did in her earlier training sessions. She didn't seem to have the same fire and grit and appeared content to "blend in" with the other horses at the racetrack. Eventually, Gritty Gal became so disinterested with training that she would stop jogging halfway around the racetrack. That's when I was called.

An Emotional Conformation Profile showed that Gritty Gal had a very high Herd Dynamic (see pp. 78 and 99). This characteristic is common to herd leaders and high-level horses in the wild. An interview with the previous owner revealed that Gritty Gal always performed better when shipped to a new racetrack than she did at her home racetrack. After looking at all the evidence, the prognosis was clear. Gritty Gal had "lost her grit" because she was no longer challenged by the everyday routine of training.

In the wild, herd leaders are challenged daily to be mentally sharp and focused in order to ensure survival of the herd, and domestic horses with a high Herd Dynamic need similar challenges to keep their edge and win on the racetrack or in the show ring. Without daily challenges, it is very easy for a horse with a high Herd Dynamic to slack off in training and become "just another horse in the herd."

I also thought there was a contributing factor: Gritty Gal had become so well adjusted to life on the farm that she had no desire to be a racehorse. On the farm, Gritty Gal had fun and was free to roam the pastures with the other horses. She now resented any restrictions to that freedom. Loading into the trailer, getting fitted with tack, and jogging around the racetrack were at odds with the life she had come to enjoy back home.

The Solution

The therapy for Gritty Gal was twofold: she needed to be given challenges to keep her focused and engaged in the training program, and she needed to begin to see training as fun and exciting rather than restrictive. The owner had a starting gate on the farm property that was used for training purposes, so we moved it to the entrance of the pasture where Gritty Gal liked to graze and roam with the other horses. Over the course of several days we walked the mare through the gate to the pasture. She showed no signs of resisting the gate and eagerly walked through to the land of fun and excitement on the other side.

After several sessions, we fitted Gritty Gal with tack and walked her through the gate. Again, Gritty Gal showed no signs of resistance and easily walked through the gate to the pasture on the other side. Once on the other side, her tack was removed and the mare was free to roam and graze. We did this for several days, and then finally, the owner rode Gritty Gal through the gate. Again, she showed no resistance—she had been assimilated to new experiences with the starting gate and she no longer saw it as a barrier to her freedom.

In order to make the mare's experience loading into the trailer seem new and challenging, rather than restrictive, on several occasions we loaded her into the trailer, took her to a new spot in the large pasture, and there unloaded her so she could graze. Sometimes we loaded her in the trailer, left her for a while with her hay, and then simply unloaded her. We used different trailers to add interest, and on several occasions, included an old gelding Gritty Gal had grown close to in our trailer adventures. Soon Gritty Gal showed no signs of stress or anxiety when loaded in the trailer. She had been assimilated to new experiences with the trailer, and she no longer saw it as a barrier to her freedom. On race day, Gritty Gal loaded into the trailer without any problems.

High Herd Dynamic athletes like Gritty Gal need to be challenged daily to maintain their mental sharpness and focus. Without those challenges, they can develop stress and anxiety that can affect their performance (see more about this in chapter 8, p. 105).

Behavior Triggers

Behavior triggers and the Potential Withholds they create in horses are issues that result from the interaction of the horse's associative memory trigger mechanism (see earlier discussion on p. 19). Headshyness, spooking easily, balking at entering or rushing into an arena or racetrack starting gate may well be reactions that are based on something very different from the immediate, *primary* stimulus. In other words, your horse may be hesitant or anxious not because of the *here and now,* but because of something that happened many years before. In chapter 2 (see p. 13) I gave you Federico Tesio's example of the feverish foal who was afraid of anyone wearing a white coat after a bad experience with a veterinarian, and hypothesized that when he grew older, it might be safe to say that the white coat would serve as a behavior trigger wielding a powerful affect, preventing the horse from entering the starting gate when someone in a white coat was present.

By understanding how this process works within the *basic* and *acquired instinct,* Potential Withholds can be revealed and sometimes circumvented, but they can never be completely eradicated. We must remind ourselves that we cannot treat the issue based only on the reactions of the horse—in doing that, we run the risk of causing deeper emotional wounds. However, there are ways to free the horse from the behavior triggers that prevent him from living up to his full potential. This begins with a proper investigation into the cause of the Potential Withholds, which means paying attention to the behavior of the horse, as well as understanding the environment in which the horse lives.

The equine's general magnanimity toward his human caretakers is both his saving grace and his downfall. Being so adaptable and compliant is the precipice from which the horse can fall into behavioral aberrations—for us, understanding the *how* allows us to understand the *why* of mental disorder issues caused by behavior triggers.

CASE STUDY

Rosebud: The Skittish Warmblood

The Problem

On one occasion, I received an e-mail from Mrs. Smith who wrote to me about an issue concerning her eight-year-old Dutch Warmblood mare. Mrs. Smith was an elderly, but quite capable, horsewoman who enjoyed her daily rides with Rosebud—a former dressage horse. They would often ride, alone or with friends, along the trails of Pennsylvania's backwoods and hedgerow-lined fields of corn and clover.

All was well until one day Rosebud suddenly reared, threw Mrs. Smith, and scurried off along the hedgerow of a clover field. This behavior continued about a dozen more times along the same hedgerow, but not in the same location. This happened, said Mrs. Smith, both when she went riding alone or with a friend. In each instance, neither rider was able to detect any sign of nervousness or apprehension in either of their horses as they rode along the trail prior to Rosebud's rear.

A thorough initial interview did not reveal anything out of the ordinary that could have triggered Rosebud's behavior. The fact that Rosebud only threw Mrs. Smith when they were riding along the hedgerow indicated that the hedgerow or something in that area may have been a trigger for an associative memory. I spent the better part of one day traversing the trail with Mrs. Smith and Rosebud, asking Mrs. Smith to ride along and proceed with her usual daily ride routine. The terrain and wildlife was what one might expect to see or encounter in the Pennsylvania backwoods country: groundhogs, birds, rabbits, broken limbs, and fluttering leaves clinging to their keepers in the brisk early summer breeze. Yet, there appeared to be nothing particularly unusual.

Next my investigation focused on the barn and daily farm routine. Smells, sensations, sounds of people, the radio, or other barn animals, all can be triggers of behavior resulting in Potential Withholds. This is often the direction to go when investigating a horse's Potential Withholds or sudden behavior changes. However, initially the barn environment and the daily interaction between Mrs. Smith and Rosebud did not reveal anything that could be a trigger for Rosebud's behavior. A day later, Rosebud again threw Mrs. Smith as they rode along the hedgerow. I decided it was time to take the investigation to another level. It was time to have "the talk," which is part of the Thomas Herding Technique that brings me into direct, consistent contact with the horse. During this period of constant exposure to the horse, I, in essence, *listen* to what he is trying to communicate by observing each body gesture and his reaction to the environment.

Rosebud and I became well acquainted as I followed her on her daily routine roaming and grazing in the fields of Mrs. Smith's farm. During this period, Light Touch Therapy (LTT) sessions (see p. 32) were initiated at various locations on the property, but I failed to detect abnormal stress levels at any time. Then, just before dusk, while performing LTT on Rosebud in her stall, I noticed that she began to exhibit signs of stress. When a cat entered the stall, Rosebud's stress levels spiked, although she did grow calm again when the cat rubbed against her fetlock. I thought this very curious. To hone in on the trigger of Rosebud's stress, I began a series of stimulus tests from direct to subtle, in front of her, behind her, on the sides, when she was wide awake, when her senses were heightened, while she was at rest, and when she was nearly asleep.

Slowly, but surely, the picture came into view.

After testing Rosebud's reaction to various stimuli in a number of different situations, I realized that she had been imprinted by something occurring at the bottom right of her peripheral line of sight. And that was exactly the location where the cat always entered her stall. I knew it had been a relatively recent imprint to stimuli Rosebud deemed dangerous based on the increase in her stress level. In short, Rosebud had been imprinted by something in her stall—a situation I refer to as *Assimilated Imprinting* (see p. 23). This normal function of the horse's basic survival instinct was causing her skittish behavior while riding on the trail with Mrs. Smith.

To investigate this conclusion, I needed to clean Rosebud's stall. As I rummaged through her stall with a pitchfork, I uncovered a wisp of fur. It wasn't cat fur and it certainly wasn't horse hair. Continuing with the cleanup, I found the culprit. Apparently the cat, during one of its hunts, caught a rabbit and carried the struggling quarry back to Rosebud's stall. Cats sometimes linger over and play with their prey before making the final kill, and it was there, in the stall, in the bottom right of Rosebud's peripheral line of sight where the violent act occurred. The death struggle that had occurred in Rosebud's stall was most likely the trigger of her skittish behavior on the trail with Mrs. Smith. Something along that trail, the flutter of a bird, the movement of a groundhog, or the scurrying of a rabbit dining on clover sparked the trigger of Rosebud's associative memory, reminding her of the incident in the stall.

9.3 A–C When I coach trainers who are working with young horses, I like to be an abstract observer so that I can judge where the horse is in his development based on his body language and intentions. Here horseman Bruce Anderson has made comfortable contact with a young horse in a round pen at the Pine Knoll Center for Integrated Horsemanship in Lexington, Kentucky. At first the horse "feels" the man with his ear but does not react further (A).

Anderson pushes the horse's space by taking a step forward, creating a behavioral trigger. This is okay because there was already a relationship established between man and horse. The result is the horse has been put in motion in a nonthreatening, safe manner (B).

After another session Anderson has created a comfortable line of communication. The horse is traveling in a smooth rhythm with his ear connected to the man, his leader (C). The goal of any training is first to establish a line of communication that will not be broken.

To test my theory, Rosebud and I needed to return to the trail near the hedgerow. As Rosebud walked along the trail, I threw to the ground within her right line of vision a stuffed animal in the likeness of a rabbit that I had tied to a string. Lo and behold, Rosebud acted up in a similar manner as she had several times before when Mrs. Smith was riding her.

Finally, the mystery was solved! Rosebud "spoke" to me loud and clear.

The Solution

My next task was to use Assimilated Imprinting to rebuild Rosebud's network of associations and behavior triggers. To do this, I followed Rosebud around the farm on her daily routine occasionally tossing the stuffed animal within her right line of

vision. Eventually, Rosebud became so familiar with the stuffed animal she did not react at all to its presence in her environment. Rosebud had been imprinted with a new associative memory, and there was no need to have any fear of other sudden movements that might occur in the bottom right of her line of sight.

Handling and Training Protocols

How the horse is handled and trained makes all the difference between success and failure in competition. Great care must be taken when the young horse enters into training. It is important to know both the physical and emotional limitations of your young horse if you hope to successfully train him to compete on the racetrack or in the show ring. The way a horse is handled and trained can, indeed, become a Potential Withhold when it involves pushing and forcing the horse to do things he is not yet physically or mentally able to do. Also, training programs that fail to push the horse enough can be a Potential Withhold, resulting in a mediocre equine athlete. (I discuss my training theories in detail in chapter 8, beginning on p. 105.)

An Emotional Conformation Profile can give you a clear picture of the performance potential of your horse and enable you to establish a training program designed to develop him into a good equine athlete (figs. 9.3 A–C). On the physical level, each horse grows at his own pace. In the same way, emotionally, some horses are quick to learn while others take time to develop. Trying to push and force the young horse to do what you want will only have disastrous results; failing to challenge him fares no better.

Great care must also be taken in handling the older horse who may have developed some bad habits from his experience with previous handlers and trainers. Trying, by force or repetition, to *train it out of him* may achieve some short-term success; however, it's not the best formula for success in the long run. You can put dirt over the fire, but it may flare up at any moment in the future, lying in wait for the right moment, the right *trigger,* to show its ugly flames.

This is a classic description of a mental Potential Withhold and the severity of its force and impact can vary widely. Maybe your horse is jittery at the gate, slow to start, or drops off at the end of a race, but during workouts, clips off impressive times. Maybe your horse schools his dressage test perfectly at home, jumps clear in training, and performs jaw-dropping stops in reining practice, only failing to perform during competition, when "it counts." The horse may repeat a task, simple or difficult, any number of times, but when you most need him to nail it, he falters. Often, it is the very simple, minor details and easy tasks that we find to be the most potent of the Potential Withholds, and they are often caused by handling or training protocols, past or present. All too often in such cases, the horse is chalked up as one full of promise but largely underachieving.

CASE STUDY

Violet: The "Washed-Up" Thoroughbred

The Problem

Violet is a good example of a racehorse that was not properly handled by her trainer. When I met her she was a seven-year-old Thoroughbred from Texas, and during her racing career she had been a very consistent and competitive runner. But in her seventh year she wasn't performing as well, and her trainer turned her over to her owner claiming she was "washed up." Joe, the owner, believed Violet still had some good racing in her and was not about to give up on a horse who had been so good to him in the past.

Not knowing what to do or where to go to get help for Violet, Joe searched the Internet for any information he could find on how to train and care for the older racehorse, and he found my website. Intrigued, he gave me a call to see if I could help his mare.

After listening to Joe's story, I told him I'd help, but it was a challenge! Joe literally was the owner of a one-horse stable in Texas and had limited resources while my office is located in Pennsylvania. The best way to proceed with Violet's case was for me to review as much historical information and film footage of Violet as Joe could send me.

After a few days of reviewing the material and film footage, I was convinced that while her previous training kept her physically in the game, the training program had not provided enough mental challenges to keep Violet interested in racing. Violet had matured and her mental aptitude outgrew her physical challenges. My prognosis? She still had some good racing days left. Physically, Violet was fit enough to be competitive and even excel at racing, but mentally, she was not involved in her races and we had to change that.

The Solution

After a basic Emotional Conformation Profile, I designed a one-month, patterns-of-motion playbook for Joe to use in training Violet. Horses in the wild learn best while in motion—that's nature's way of ensuring survival. Likewise, equine athletes learn how to be good performers when competing. With that as a template, Mental Stimulus Exercises were implemented to retrain Violet the basics of how to run and remain engaged throughout a race.

Patterns of behavior are reflected within patterns of motion, and it was important for Violet to learn how to control her own motion when running in a race and anticipate the motion of other horses. Part of the playbook strategy called for the creation of a 6-mile *Mental Stimulus Course* where Joe could work Violet and train her how to increase her Focus Agility during a prolonged period of time-in-motion (see p. 43). It's important for such focus training to be during a prolonged period of time because that is what strengthens *the mental capacity of the equine to control the physical output of the athlete.* The ability to remain focused during competition is extremely important for the equine athlete to be a successful competitor.

A month after I had created a playbook for Violet an excited Joe called me. "Kerry, its working!" he said. "She's moving with energy I've not seen before!" I encouraged Joe to keep training Violet with Mental Stimulus Exercises to keep her focused and engaged during training. It appeared that Violet had really begun to blossom. If her Focus Agility continued to improve, and she continued to move forward in her training, there was a good possibility that racing and the thrill of competition would once more become exciting for the "washed-up" Thoroughbred.

Behavioral Overcompensation

Behavioral overcompensation can be a devastating Potential Withhold for the sport horse and occurs when the equine athlete alters his natural movement style due to a physical or an emotionally-perceived restriction, resulting in a loss of the athlete's efficiency of motion. Track or ring surface and condition, blinkers, shadow rolls, and the tack a horse wears (whether it fits, whether it causes discomfort) are a few examples of physical restrictions that can cause the horse to alter his natural movement style (fig. 9.4). A horse relies on his senses for survival, and when a horse is fitted with equipment that restricts one of his senses or causes him to feel emotionally inhibited, the horse will do things to adjust or overcompensate for that restriction, and that overcompensation can often have a negative effect on the horse's pattern of motion.

Emotional restrictions can stem from experiences on the racetrack or in the show pen, such as when the horse has been banged and jostled about by other horses or livestock, resulting in cautious or timid behavior. The horse has to feel comfortable and have confidence in order to perform at peak levels. Being forced to race or perform can also cause behavioral overcompensation—anything, physical or emotional, real or anticipated, that restricts the horse's freedom of movement can result in behavioral overcompensation, and it is one of the toughest challenges for domesticated horses to overcome.

Behavioral Overcompensation and Speed

There is a steep set of basement steps in my older home, yet I can swiftly traverse them, up or down, without any fear of falling when all of my senses— including vision, touch, and hearing—are in play. However, on laundry day I cautiously walk down the stairs because my vision is obstructed by the large basket full of clothes I'm carrying. I still make it safely down the steps, but I have to *overcompensate* for the lack of vision by using my feet to help guide me to the bottom of the stairs. I complete the same distance from the top of the stairs to the washing machine; however, I do so in a slower time-in-motion. A good example of this is when the racehorse experiences mud kickback on a sloppy track—a lot of horses overcompensate on a sloppy track.

Behavior Overcompensation and Pace

When prolonged time-in-motion is combined with speed, the efficiency with which a given distance is covered is ultimately controlled by the horse's Focus Agility. If you think of it like a relay race where a baton is passed from hand to hand, the

Kerry's Corner

Question: **What are your thoughts in regards to a horse needing to or being made to wear blinkers on the racetrack? Is this—in reality—an impediment to the horse in the long run, as opposed to the short-term supposed gains?** —Martha, England

Answer: I feel it is a fallacy to think one will attain consistent success by limiting or inhibiting any of the equine senses. A horse should be guided into his athletic environment with all of the senses nature has equipped him with fully intact. The constriction of one sense only leads to the eventual heightening of the other senses, and during this process, while the body assimilates to this change, a great deal of stress is necessarily incurred. This leads to many other collateral issues and may do more harm than good in the long run.

I feel that if a racehorse requires a "training aid" such as blinkers to focus on the task before him, or in essence needs to be *separated* from the Herd Dynamics that develop during the group in motion, you have a generic, inconsistent racehorse. The question that should be asked is: How ready to race is the horse, win or lose? To me, it makes more sense to develop training protocols that embrace and utilize the natural senses in *all* of their capacities. Sensory training is a very important part of the overall picture (far too often overlooked) and is essential in developing the *mentally sound equine*. A horse fully aware of his environment and who is allowed full use of the senses has a greater ability to swiftly interpret his individual place within the group, whether a herd in motion as is the case in a race, or within a casual pasture setting.

first leg of the race will always be started by reaction and speed. Yet as the time-in-motion protracts and the burst of physical energy wanes, a different strategy is employed to maintain motion—the baton is handed over from the hand of speed to the hand of pace. Focus thus becomes the determining factor of the efficiency with which physical distance is covered. This means that during a race you can have two horses, side-by-side, covering the same distance of ground, each with exactly equal physical ability, but the two horses can have different time-in-motion. The determining factor between them, if indeed each horse is physically equal, is *their individual ability to manage the time they are in motion.* The further the distance, the more a horse is less reliant on pure speed and more reliant on Focus Agility, which determines pace (see more about this on p. 114).

The most important factor for the equine athlete is to perform with peak efficiency of motion. If your horse does not transition well, or swiftly, he is not being efficient, and you are not getting the most from his ability. Mental training, mental nurturing, and improving the horse's ability to focus are the keys to developing efficiency of his motion.

9.4 Behavioral overcompensation can be a serious impediment to the equine athlete, causing poor performance during competition. Here the lead horse is worrying too much about what is behind him, partly because the blinkers are inhibiting his senses. The result is his pattern of motion becomes disrupted, negatively affecting his rhythm and efficiency, and ultimately his ability to win.

CASE STUDY

Friesian: The Hesitant Dressage Horse

The Problem

The case of Friesian is a good illustration of how a behavior trigger can cause the horse to have behavioral overcompensations. One day I received a telephone call from a horse owner who had recently purchased a fine Friesian stallion to compete in dressage. Both the horse and rider had considerable experience in dressage, and the owner had high hopes for her recent purchase. However, as the owner worked with Friesian, she discovered that he had some behavioral issues. An interesting one was that whenever the two of them faced a wall (say, of the indoor) while performing piaffe, his collection seemed hesitant. Smooth transitions and patterns of motion are important for the dressage horse to be a successful competitor; hesitation or awkward, jerky movements will quickly get you a low score from the judges. The owner had a serious problem on her hands and did not know how to fix it. I agreed to meet with her and do an Emotional Conformation Profile of Friesian.

Hesitation in movement is a sure sign of a behavioral issue, and it can take some time to properly diagnose the cause of the problem. Two things I look for when profiling a horse with behavioral issues are: behavior triggers (what, exactly, could be the cause of the hesitant behavior—see p. 135), and any signs of behavioral overcompensation (the things a horse will do when one of his senses is inhibited by an emotional restriction or by equipment such as blinkers, ear plugs or muffs, and even tack).

The Emotional Conformation Profile gave me a good idea of Friesian's space of influence. That is to say, the profile gave me a good idea of Friesian's focus range and how far away he detected changes to space infractions. A series of tests quickly revealed that Friesian had space issues and that influences or objects close near the side and at ground level were major problem areas for the otherwise efficient athlete. Further investigation was done in various forms of testing the space interpretation of Friesian—both blind spots and visual. The visual aspects were sketchy but created a pretty consistent, decreased response to space infraction. This is to be expected in such cases, but the real problem for Friesian was in the area of his blind spots, where anticipation of any stimulus whatsoever seemed to have a paralyzing grip on him, stifling any hope for higher levels of dressage competition.

What I found was that any change, either real or perceived, to stimuli in that sensitive area created an exaggerated response, altering his next move—if only for a split second. Repeated testing of Friesian with variable stimuli created similar results, indicating that an incident or experience from Friesian's past became an associative memory, which served as a trigger of his hesitant behavior when he encountered or perceived changes in objects or stimuli at his near side and at ground level. Whenever Friesian experienced similar situations, whether real or imagined, he would always move in the same hesitant manner—until that associative memory could be assimilated with a new (nonthreatening) life experience.

The Solution

To help Friesian overcome his hesitation of movement, the goal was to assimilate him to new experiences that he viewed as nonthreatening using the THT AirWorks System, which uses *patterns of behavior* to nurture *patterns of motion* (see more about this in chapter 8, p. 105). For Friesian to efficiently manage his space while in motion he needed to be taught how to adjust his behavior so that his influence and focus of attention were on far away objects rather than on objects near his side and at ground level.

A good analogy of how this works is when you are walking along and constantly staring at your feet. Your range of influence and focus is concentrated on every step you take. The ease and fluidity of your motion is greatly hampered by short, choppy steps, and when you encounter an object in your path you hesitate or quickly dodge it (overcompensate) to get out of its way. Its only when you finally cast your gaze on the far horizon that you are able to see everything in sight, lengthen your stride, and improve your ease and fluidity of motion.

This applied to Friesian. By extending Friesian's range of influence and focus, nearby objects would no longer have a paralyzing effect or cause him to be hesitant when performing. To accomplish this, Mental Stimulus Exercises were implemented that would help Friesian learn how to extend his range of influence and focus attention.

Equine Cabin Fever

In the artificial, domesticated environment, many horses spend a good portion of their life confined in a stall where there is little room to move. This confinement, especially in the case of the convalescing horse, can be a Potential Withhold and a source of stress, resulting in what I refer to as *Equine Cabin Fever*—a form of mental illness. Over time, Equine Cabin Fever can lead to serious levels of depression and psychosis in the horse. The initial symptoms of Equine Cabin Fever cover

9.5 A & B Providing the horse with companions, in the barn and in the pasture, is a good way to offset the effects of Equine Cabin Fever. Other horses (A), or sheep, goats, and chickens (B), can help keep a bored, confined horse mentally stimulated.

a wide range of odd activities, including pacing, chewing, head-bobbing, weaving, and wind-sucking, among many others. In extreme cases, the horse may even lash out at his handler.

If you have ever been confined to a bed because of sickness or injury, then you may have an idea of what Equine Cabin Fever is like for the horse. Like the horse in the stall, your freedom of movement has been restricted. Your normal, everyday routine has been disrupted. You have places to go to and things you'd like to do, but you are unable. You are alone and often consumed with little other than the thought of how to escape your confinement.

When someone comes into the room to give you medicine or attend to your injury, you may be harsh with them. That behavior is completely unlike your normal character. But, you cannot help yourself because you are not your normal self—you are convalescing. The caregiver can come and go but you cannot. The hours, days pass by. Relief does not come. Eventually you may talk to yourself to relieve the anxiety and stave off depression. Perhaps you amuse yourself by cracking your knuckles repeatedly. The situation is not hard to imagine, and not unlike the pacing, head-bobbing horse in the stall.

The best preventive step to ward off Equine Cabin Fever is to allow the horse as much pasture time with others as possible. The Natural Herd Dynamic is nurtured by time spent in the pasture, and the horse will be better adjusted and more mentally sound when he is allowed turnout. When the horse must be confined to the barn, then the next best preventive measure is to provide a lot of daily mental stimulation. Take the horse out of his stall and walk in the barn aisle. Move the horse to a different stall at the opposite end of the barn. Change his feed location. Provide goats, sheep, or chickens, and other horses as companions (figs. 9.5 A & B). Note that I never use dogs or cats as sole babysitters for horses during long periods of confinement. During confinement, the horse's natural instinct of survival is heightened, and no matter how well behaved the dog or cat, by nature they are predators. The last thing you want in a barn full of horses already on edge is a real or imaginary altercation with a predator.

All of the steps I've outlined can help the horse to stay mentally active and ward off the symptoms of Equine Cabin Fever.

CASE STUDY

Home on the Range
The Problem

In the winter of 2002 during one of my research expeditions studying the wild Mustang, I took a short break to visit with a fellow named Wesley—a friend of my cousin. Little did I know that my "short break" would end up being a two-week sleepover! A freezing rain blew in from the Rocky Mountains, covering the entire region in a thick sheet of ice, which later changed into a blanket of snow—a devilish mix making movement, human or equine, extremely hazardous. Out West, winter storms can occur with little warning, and we barely had time to round up Wesley's seven Quarter Horses from the range where they had been grazing before the bad weather set in.

For several months, Wesley's horses had roamed the range steadily, and they never spent more than two nights inside his barn. It had small stalls and was used primarily to store feed and equipment. The ice and snow made it necessary that the horses remain stabled, but after three days in the barn, all seven started to show signs of emotional stress. I knew they would be able to more easily manage their physical confinement if we could provide emotional or mental stimulation.

The Solution

At that time, and still today, there are a lot of "horse toys" on the market, such as balls, roll stands, and pacifiers, which are intended to relieve boredom and stress in the stabled equine. However, Wesley didn't have any of these toys because Mother Nature provided his horses with the daily natural nurturing necessary for good mental health. Instead, Wesley and I spent a lot of time grooming and walking them up and down the aisle of the barn. We also tied "streamers" from the rafters—long strands of ribbon that hung at various lengths and softly danced in the wind of the drafty old barn, tickling heads and withers.

When horses are confined in stalls for long periods, they can become overprotective of their space and resent any real or perceived intrusion from strangers. By the sixth day of confinement, the Quarter Horses had ceased being overprotective of their space and had settled into a depressed mood of acceptance. The ribbons had lost their stimulating effect—like the abandoned toys a child has become bored with—and it became necessary to provide other means of mental activity. Inanimate objects will only go so far in giving horses what they need to promote good mental health, and during extended periods of confinement, it becomes necessary to provide horses with *living* sources of mental stimulation.

So Wesley and I turned some chickens loose in the barn to keep the horses company. The chickens were the only other source of livestock on the farm, and by day nine, they had done a good job pacifying the horses.

Finally, on the tenth day, we were able to turn the horses out and allow them the freedom and ability to roam that nature intended.

Human Attachment Disorder

The horse was born to run free in the wild, but the awesome ability of the horse to adapt to different environs allows him to also live quite comfortably in the domestic environment. However, the price the performance horse pays for this adaptability is sometimes not seen until late in his life when he has lost his "usefulness" and is sold or retired.

Confined in a stall for most of his hours with too little equine contact in the pasture, the horse assimilates to this unnatural environment and can develop a strong bond to his human caretaker as his *bandmate.* This bonding occurs because, as a herding animal, horses are social creatures. In this scenario, the normal Natural Herd Dynamic and bonding with other herd horses has been replaced by the horse's interaction with his handler—whether his groom, owner, rider, or trainer.

While in training, the horse receives constant care and attention from his primary handler, and he is completely dependent on the handler for his well-being. When the horse is sold or retired, this human-equine circle is broken, which can have a profound effect on the horse, resulting in what I refer to as Human Attachment Disorder.

Human Attachment Disorder is one of the most deplorable and troublesome psychological issues experienced by the horse, and it can be especially bad for the sport horse in retirement. For years, the horse has been pampered, cared for, and attended to by his handler, and then one day, the horse is no longer the center of attention. After years of being stalled on his own with primarily humans to interact with, suddenly the horse is turned out in a field with other horses. The new experience can produce a very high degree of stress and worry for the horse as he adapts to his new environment.

The older the horse, the harder it is for him to adapt to a new life without the regularity of training for competition. In this instance, enrichment type therapies must be put in place that will help him adjust. It is not unlike trying to teach the orphaned bear cub to find his own food and shelter. Removed from his previous, pampered, sheltered environment, the horse is, in essence, an orphan of sorts. Without the natural social order of the Herd Dynamic in place, it is his surrogate family that must do the teaching.

This is a serious issue if we are truly to rehabilitate the retired horse. Often I am called upon to profile prospective horses for people who are interested in adopting or buying a former equine athlete who has been retired from competition due to injury or old age. I've seen a wide variety of horses—barrel racers, racehorses, jumpers, and dressage horses—from different athletic training backgrounds make the transition from competition to retirement on the farm. The outcome of that transition is usually the same in every case—the physical transition is much easier for the horse than the mental transition. The emotional impact of environmental disruptions and lifestyle changes needs to be fully understood if one is to properly maintain the physical and mental health of the horse. Without emotional wellness, physical health is tainted, the Equine Circle is broken.

In my study of the horse I have found that how he handles his life experiences is often similar to and reflective of how humans handle their own experiences.

THT Reflective Learning Therapy:
Using Horses to Promote Healing and Emotional Wellness in Humans

The Thomas Herding Technique Reflective Learning Therapy program is designed to introduce and educate therapists to the benefits of using horses when working with children with physical and emotional challenges. Many therapy programs that use horses are designed to promote *physical* health; Reflective Learning Therapy (RLT) promotes emotional health, as well.

Horses tell us things about ourselves, and about others, by the way they react to our approach, our stance, our frame of mind. Horses can act as "mirrors" of our emotions. They read our intent, our body language, and immediately know far more about us than we would often like the world to know! But this is also a powerful tool—a cathartic, therapeutic journey of emotional wellness based within interspecies communication. The horse is an ally in our quest for wellness. Communication is a key to learning more about ourselves and each other, and the horse is a great communicator.

The same communication tools used to develop and nurture the equine athlete can be used to define and nurture the human in reflection. Perhaps the greatest gift the horse has to share with us is not on the racetrack or in the dressage ring, but rather as teacher, a guide on an internal journey. Because the horse "reflects" our emotions (whether we want him to or not) he can provide vital information about our inner calm or inner turmoil, our sadness or our elation, our feelings of love or loathing. I have used this in developing interactive programs for children struggling with disadvantages, such as blindness or autism. The horse serves as a great translator of children's unexpressed emotions, both good and bad, and inasmuch becomes the "emotional voice" for those who cannot, or who refuse to speak.

Using an equine-assisted therapy program based on Herd Dynamics and equine communication allows the therapist to monitor the progress of the children participating, establish a platform for their development, and reference a unique reflective learning protocol with the horse as the translator. The horse can open the door for emotional growth and well-being— learning to "read" the language of the horse, and allowing oneself to be read, can open an otherwise concealed path to human wellness.

From that study, I developed what I call *Reflective Learning Therapy (RLT),* which is built upon the idea that horses "reflect" human emotion (they are "mirrors to our soul," it is said). Horses read our intent and our body language, and serve as a great translator of unexpressed emotion—good and bad. They can serve as an "emotional voice" for those who cannot, or refuse to speak. RLT can, therefore, be used with great success to help physically and mentally disadvantaged children deal with their daily challenges (see sidebar).

Because of this reflective nature that exists between horse and man, sometimes it is easier to understand the impact of environmental and lifestyle changes on the Equine Circle when compared to circumstances in our own world. As a child, dependent on your parents for your care and well-being, you may have experienced the pain and loss of friendship when your parents moved the family to a new community. Perhaps you were pulled out of school, away from your best friend and favorite teachers, and placed in a new one where you were surrounded by strangers. Do you remember how this may have seemed like a traumatizing experience? Do you remember the pang of missing your best friend? Perhaps pining after your old hangouts? In such a situation, it can take a long time to adjust, if you ever adjust, to your new environment. You might be physically "there," but mentally, you are still "back home."

This is not unlike what the horse experiences when sold or retired after a competitive career with one handler, trainer, or rider.

CASE STUDY

Ruby Red: A Horse in Transition
The Problem

I came to know a kind mare named Ruby Red—a retired Quarter Horse who became attached to an elderly lady named Betsy. For 10 years Ruby Red was the sole equine occupant in Betsy's spacious backyard. She was completely dependent on Betsy for her care and well-being, and Betsy pampered Ruby Red, day after day. Over the years, the pair developed a strong bond of friendship. Ruby Red was the center of Betsy's attention.

Finally, the day came when Betsy, getting on in age, reluctantly sold Ruby Red to another farm whose owner had plans to use her as a therapy horse. The new owner thought that Ruby Red, being an older, lonely mare, would enjoy the company of other horses and fit in nicely with her stable of seven. To her chagrin, that was not the case. For the first time in 10 years, Ruby Red was miserable, and it showed in her daily attitude on the farm. The mare wouldn't associate or go near the other horses and could often be found standing alone in the paddock or pasture. At feeding time, she would wait for the other horses to get their fill of hay and would only feed when the others wandered off. Ruby Red was no longer the center of someone's attention. Like the child transferred to a new school, Ruby Red had made the physical transition to the new farm but, mentally, she was still grazing in Betsy's spacious backyard.

That's when I was called in to see if I could help Ruby Red adjust to her new environment. Horses like Ruby Red who've lived much of their life in solitude, for the most part separate from other horses and a herd environment, need to be taught by their handlers how to, in essence, *be a horse*. Horses interact via a complex communication network (see chapter 7, p. 89) that ensures self-preservation and survival of the herd. But horses like Ruby Red, who have been exposed very little to other horses, do not know how to "speak the language," and they can take a while to learn how to fit in and communicate.

The Solution

Because horses learn best when in motion, I developed a patterns-of-motion therapy program to help Ruby Red learn how to interact and understand the intentions of the other horses in the stable. Feeding time is a great opportunity to work with horses with behavioral problems, so we walked Ruby Red behind another horse as he made his way to where the hay had been placed in the paddock. Ruby Red's comfort zone was about three lengths behind the other horse, and that was okay. While the goal was to get her to feed with the other horses, pushing Ruby Red out of her comfort zone would have been counterproductive.

After a few sessions, Ruby Red was walked beside the other horse on the way to feed. On other occasions, different paths were taken to get to the hay, but she was still cued by a human to join the other horses as they ate.

This "feeding time therapy" continued for about a month, and at the end of "communication school" Ruby Red was associating and interacting with the other horses as though they were lifelong friends.

Equine Abandonment Syndrome

Equine Abandonment Syndrome is one of the most difficult behavioral disorders to diagnose because many of the symptoms are similar to those of Human Attachment Disorder (see p. 148). With both disorders, the horse often suffers a sense of loss and abandonment from his human handlers. But with Equine Abandonment Syndrome, the horse also feels a sense of being left by a herd, or he misses a pasture, a barn, or a particular lifestyle—such as that of a competitive racehorse or show horse. This happens because the horse is a social animal and forms attachments to his environment. When those attachments are severed, the horse can develop emotional aberrations that can affect his mental and physical condition. Cribbing or weaving, withdrawal and depression, signs of being overly protective of space and even meanness are just a few of the symptoms horses display when afflicted with Equine Abandonment Syndrome. Because of the similarities with signs of Human Attachment Disorder, a correct diagnosis can only be reached after an Emotional Conformation Profile (see p. 78) and an extensive investigation of the horse's history.

Any horse can experience Equine Abandonment Syndrome but it mostly occurs in equine athletes who, after several years of competition, feel a sudden sense of loss and abandonment when retired. Some equine athletes, especially the good ones, can get attached or "addicted" to the excitement and thrill of competition, and when retired can suffer from severe behavioral problems. For the retired horse, Equine Abandonment Syndrome is a more deeply rooted onset of what I term *social distortion,* which can be of minor consequence in outbursts akin to the weaning process. Or it can protract and expand into various levels of depression, with a growing number of other farm animals and humans viewed with less and less favor. The more the horse is withdrawn, the deeper the depression. The deeper the depression, or *syndrome,* the fewer accepted associates and the horse eventually becomes isolated. Like us, horses can show signs of isolation even when amidst a crowd. Isolating oneself is first a mental transition and isn't always accompanied by obvious detachment from others. It is also true that *inanimate things,* which are easier to control than *living things,* can replace communication and intimate relationships—this is both a human and an observed equine propensity.

Equine Abandonment Syndrome can also occur during weaning when the young horse and mare are separated. As we've discussed, when not handled properly, weaning can become a Potential Withhold that has a detrimental effect on the horse for the rest of his life (see p. 127). Untreated, Equine Abandonment Syndrome can result in mental illness.

CASE STUDY

Pay Attention—Learning to Like a Life of Leisure

The Problem

I was contacted on Facebook in the spring of 2011 to see if I could help a woman named Amanda who had fallen in love with a Thoroughbred when she watched him race one day at Penn National Race Course. Amanda had purchased the horse (named Pay Attention) when the owner retired him in 2009. Pay Attention was a gelding, and as is often common practice for the gelded racehorse, he was kept in competition until the age of eight.

Retirement for humans in the United States is part of the "American Dream." It promises the "golden years" that every hard-working citizen hopes and dreams of one day having—but after several months of leisure, many people find adjusting to the quietude of retirement difficult or boring. They find themselves taking a part-time job or doing volunteer work to keep from going crazy.

Like some humans, Pay Attention found retirement difficult. On the farm where Amanda boarded him, he had to be kept separate from the other horses because he was overly protective of his space. Whenever other horses were in the same pasture with Pay Attention, he would target and charge them. If an inanimate object was in the paddock or pasture with him, he would charge it, too. When Amanda came to visit, Pay Attention would not charge her, but he moved toward her in a more forceful manner than that of other horses. The severity of Pay Attention's maladjustment was not clearly evident until one day he bucked off a rider in a terrifying manner. That's when I was called in to see if I could help the horse adjust to his life of leisure.

The "Charge! Charge! Charge!" mentality is commonly developed by career racehorses like Pay Attention, who are accustomed to competing to pass other horses and cross the finish line first. However, it doesn't work in the tranquil farm environment comprised of barns, paddocks, and pastures. Pay Attention had to be taught how to assimilate to his new environment. An Emotional Conformation Profile revealed that mentally Pay Attention was an above average horse in terms of mental capacity, so I thought he would be teachable.

The Solution

Horses like Pay Attention who spend much of their life in training and competition often lack the communication and interactive skills that other horses acquire from their daily interaction in the herd environment. So, because horses learn best while in motion, I developed a series of patterns-of-motion exercises to help Pay Attention learn those skills.

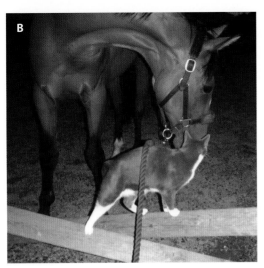

9.6 A–C Through the use of a longe line, retired Thoroughbred racehorse Pay Attention learned to communicate with his handler as he adjusted to his new environment away from the intensity of the racetrack (A). Once extremely overprotective of his space, patterns-of-motion exercises helped Pay Attention become friendly with people and animals (B). He has successfully transitioned to his new lifestyle and is a happy, social horse (C).

At first the exercises were performed in an indoor arena where Pay Attention could be walked in a controlled environment. He was introduced to inanimate objects placed in front of him and along the sides of his path. The purpose of the exercise was to help Pay Attention understand that he was in a safe environment and didn't need to use forceful body language to investigate and control inanimate objects.

At first, Pay Attention would lose focus while walking in the ring, and he wanted to charge the objects when he viewed them from a distance. But as the training progressed he eventually focused on walking on the path and was less inclined to charge the inanimate objects. The next phase was to take Pay Attention outside and repeat the training exercise in the open environment of the paddock and pasture. Once the gelding successfully completed this phase of therapy, he was on his way to assimilating to his life of leisure. To further adjust Pay Attention to his new environment, he was given a lot of pasture time, often in the company of an old, seasoned mare. Although accepting his new environment and schedule will continue to be a daily learning lesson for Pay Attention, thanks to the love and skills of Amanda, the future looks bright (figs. 9.6 A–C).

Equine "Life Coaching"

An investigation into the psyche of your horse and the environment that is influencing his senses will often reveal the Potential Withholds preventing him from living up to his fullest potential. In order to effectively "cleanse" the horse of emotional disorders, behavioral enrichment therapies must slowly be put in place. Without therapy, the strangling grip of Potential Withholds are almost impossible to pry away, and they can have a devastating effect on your equine athlete. For the horse dealing with behavior disorders, the development of leadership-stylized enrichment and socialization therapies goes far in "freeing" the horse from his issues. Continued work in this area (I discuss some aspects of this kind of training in chapter 8, beginning on p. 105) effectively serves as "life coaching" for the horse—we do it for other athletes, so why not the equine competitor?

Embracing the Magic within the Spirit of the Horse: A Final Case Study

"If we wish to return the full measure of what the horse has given us, then we must look beyond our world and do our utmost to provide opportunity for the horse to flourish."

Our journey is almost complete. You have entered into the Equine Circle and learned to embrace "the magic within the spirit of the horse." You have witnessed the effects of Potential Withholds and Equine Mental Illness and how they can have a devastating effect on the domestic horse. You have grown to understand the importance of nurturing the Natural Herd Dynamic in an artificial, domestic environment for the development of emotionally and physically fit, sound performance horses. You have seen the importance of Emotional Conformation Profiling in breeding, buying, and training horses. You discovered the Communicated Equine and learned how establishing a playbook in order to train the "emotional" horse, as well as the physical horse can be the key to a performance horse's success.

Before we part company, though, I would like to share with you one last case study. I did not work on this case, but in all my years of research and study, this horse, more than any other horse, epitomizes the negative, destructive impact of Potential Withholds and mental illness in the equine athlete, and ultimately, triumph over those destructive forces. This horse has been deceased for many years now, but in his day, this Thoroughbred—a racehorse—suffered from many of the Potential Withholds and exhibited many of the symptoms of Equine Mental Illness I've described in this book (see chapter 9, p. 125).

This horse lived in a very restrictive environment, spending much of his time cooped up in stalls or in a railroad freight car when he was not racing. Confined in such a way, the horse suffered from serious bouts of depression and spent much of his time pacing back and forth in his stall. The result was he got little sleep and ate even less. The horse developed a mean disposition and when anyone ventured near his stall, he would lunge at them like a wild, savage beast.

On race day, getting the horse ready for the start was always a struggle, and the horse would throw a fit when entering the gate. Once the bell rang, however, all fight would leave him, and the horse would often put forth a lackluster, mediocre performance on the track, although on rare occasions, he would win a race.

The horse was constantly shipped from one racetrack to another. In the course of one exhaustive year during his two-year-old season, the young Thoroughbred was shipped over 6,000 miles and competed in an astounding 35 races—a schedule that would more than test the mettle of a mature racehorse.

By halfway through his season as a three-year-old, the horse had only managed to win seven races in 44 lifetime starts, with eight second-place finishes and six third-place finishes. The horse's owners had lost all hope of him ever amounting to much and looked for a prospective buyer. Life, indeed, had been a hard one thus far for this horse. His future looked bleak, and his days as a racehorse appeared to be numbered—until a very special trainer came along. Then, everything changed.

The name of this horse was Seabiscuit.

10.1 Trainer Tom Smith saw a spark of "something" in Seabiscuit when he watched him race at Suffolk Downs in East Boston, Massachusetts. Smith knew how to "embrace the magic within the spirit of the horse," and he wanted Seabiscuit for his string.

Seabiscuit: A Tale of Hope and Courage

Like Federico Tesio, Tom Smith knew how to embrace the magic within the spirit of the horse, and that is how he turned a down-and-out, neglected, and ragged horse by the name of Seabiscuit into a champion Thoroughbred and the hero of a nation (fig. 10.1).

Seabiscuit came to the stable of Tom Smith in the summer of 1936, and over the course of two-and-a-half years, Smith transformed Seabiscuit from a low-level, mediocre, racehorse into a champion and the 1938 Horse of the Year. Seabiscuit is most famously known for winning the 1940 Santa Anita "Hundred Grander" Handicap—which at that time, was the richest horserace in the world—and for defeating his close relative War Admiral (the 1937 Triple Crown winner and Horse of the Year) in a match race—the 1938 Pimlico Special.

During the latter part of the depression-era 1930s, Seabiscuit was a sports superstar. He lived like one, too. By the end of his racing career, Seabiscuit had traveled 50,000 miles by railroad, from one end of the country to the other. Along the way, he won one race after another, setting numerous track records. Wherever Seabiscuit appeared, thousands of horseracing fans, from all walks of life, gathered to get a glimpse of him. Whenever Seabiscuit raced, it was as if the world stood still. Everyone that could not make it to the track gathered around the radio to listen to the call of the race. (It is even said that on one occasion, President Franklin Delano Roosevelt skipped an important staff meeting in order to listen to a broadcast of one of Seabiscuit's races.)

In theaters around the country, newsreels showed movie footage of Seabiscuit's races. Newspapers and magazines headlined his exploits on the racetrack. In the course of one year, the horse received more press coverage than Roosevelt, Benito Mussolini, and Adolph Hitler. Seabiscuit was so loved and admired, he became the "everyman," the "little guy who made good," to a nation of poverty-stricken people, desperately searching for hope.

The "Ugly Duckling" in a Long Line of Champions

A Wheatley Stable homebred by the sire Hard Tack, Seabiscuit was a grandson of the legendary Man o' War—one of the greatest horses in the history of Thorough-bred horseracing. Man o' War was a grandson of Hastings, and almost all of the horses of the Hastings sire line were magnificent, sleek, swift racehorses, but ill-tempered and hard to manage—especially Hastings and Hard Tack, who terrorized their handlers on and off the racetrack.

At birth, Seabiscuit was far from magnificent. He was the smallest, puniest foal on the farm. When the owners came around one day to inspect the foal crop, the stablehands hid him from view. The one redeeming quality about Seabiscuit was that he apparently had not inherited any of his ancestors' bad manners. He was an easygoing, happy, good-natured yearling. Eating and sleeping were his favorite pastimes.

When training time rolled around, Seabiscuit was in the hands of the legendary James "Sunny Jim" Fitzsimmons, who in the 1930s was one of the most respected trainers in the country. Fitzsimmons had already trained Gallant Fox and his son Omaha to Triple Crown victories, and at the time was prepping another son of Gallant Fox, Granville, for a bid at a third Triple Crown. Granville was Fitzsimmons' top horse; he always received the best treatment.

Seabiscuit was the lowly son of Hard Tack who had been a holy terror for Fitzsimmons to train. (Fitzsimmons eventually gave up on training Hard Tack when the stallion refused to budge from the gate at the start of a race.) Despite the fact that Seabiscuit actually started in more races, set three track records, and earned more money than Granville during their two-year-old racing season, Fitzsimmons did not have a very high opinion of Seabiscuit and gave him little attention.

The Difference between a Commoner and a King

Despite his regal breeding, Seabiscuit was eventually deemed a failure on the race-track, and on his way to that outcome, somehow, somewhere, things went terribly wrong. The mild-mannered, docile, easygoing colt became a carbon copy of his ill-tempered, hard-to-handle, ancestors. And this led to his eventual sale.

When Seabiscuit came to the stable of trainer Tom Smith, he was one of the

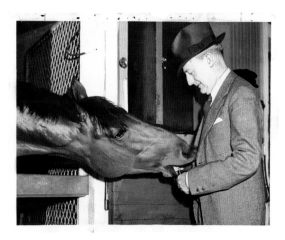

10.2 Seabiscuit only had seven wins in 44 starts when he came to the stable of Charles Howard, here shown giving Seabiscuit a treat. (Howard always treated the horse like a champion.)

most pitiful, careworn horses that Smith had ever seen. The strenuous racing schedule as a two-year-old and the long, many miles of travel across the country in railcars had taken its toll on the youngster. Despite Seabiscuit's haggard, rough-hewn appearance, Smith had seen a spark of "magic" in the horse when, while scouting horses for his new boss Charles Howard, he watched Seabiscuit win an allowance race at Suffolk Downs in East Boston, Massachusetts. Smith knew, then, that he had to have Howard add Seabiscuit to his stable (fig. 10.2).

What impressed Smith the most about Seabiscuit that day at Suffolk Downs had nothing to do with his racing record, pitiful as it was, or his conformation—Seabiscuit was a knobby-kneed, short, blunt, ragged young horse who displayed a wild thrashing and flailing of his left foreleg as he raced around the track. What caught Smith's eye was the confidence that Seabiscuit displayed as he walked around the Suffolk Downs paddock. Smith knew the difference between a "commoner" and a "king" among horses. Seabiscuit had the "look" that indicated the Emotional Conformation of a natural-born herd leader.

Smith knew that look. Since he started breaking horses at the age of 13, Smith lived, ate, and slept with horses, and he had a deep, intuitive understanding of the intimate drama of life in the Equine Circle. While he never achieved the same level of success as Federico Tesio, like the Italian breeder and trainer, Smith spent hour after hour observing and studying the horses of his stable.

Nuturing Mind and Body

Despite the horse's pitiful physical and mental condition, Smith knew he could do much with Seabiscuit after the horse was nursed back to health. First he had to heal the young horse's mind and "free" the colt from the Potential Withholds that held him back. Only by nurturing the Natural Herd Dynamic could Smith put Seabiscuit on the road to recovery.

To begin with, Smith needed to create a peaceful, stable environment for Seabiscuit to inhabit. As we discussed earlier in this book, the environment is the foundation, the bedrock upon which all great breeding and training programs originate—remember Burchard von Oettingen's Royal Trakehnen Stud and Federico Tesio's Dormello, nestled in the hills on beautiful Lake Miaggiore (see pp. 48 and 52).

In order to make Seabiscuit's environment more inviting and as natural as possible, Smith had his stall lined with a special dust-free rice straw, and the horse was fed a steady diet of oats and Timothy hay, rich in calcium to repair and strengthen tired, damaged bones. On the road, Seabiscuit traveled from one racetrack to another in a specially modified railcar that was half full of the dust-free rice straw for ample bedding while the other half was clear so the horse had plenty of room to move around and get exercise. On those trips, Smith slept in the same railcar with Seabiscuit, and he gave him daily walks in the cleared area as the train clickity-clacked down the track.

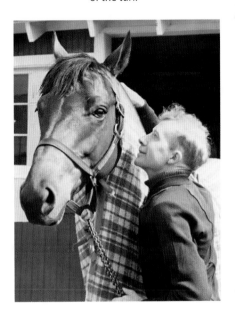

10.3 Tom Smith personally picked jockey John "Red" Pollard to ride Seabiscuit. That decision proved fateful as the two would become legends of the turf.

For peace of mind and to relieve the stress that had consumed Seabiscuit during his exhaustive racing campaign as a two-year-old, Smith provided equine companionship in the form of a lead horse he often used by the name of Pumpkin. This was one of the best ways to heal any symptoms of Equine Cabin Fever that Seabiscuit had developed while cooped up in stalls at racetracks and in railroad cars. Seabiscuit and Pumpkin became immediate friends. Smith put Pumpkin in an adjoining stall and knocked out the separating wall, and wherever Seabiscuit went, Pumpkin accompanied him.

Triumph Found

Life, indeed, was good to Seabiscuit at Charles and Marcela Howard's Ridgewood Farm. The Howards, Smith, Red Pollard (the jockey who rode Seabiscuit in many of his important races), and Ollie, the stable-hand, loved and pampered the horse day and night (fig. 10.3). They nurtured the Natural Herd Dynamic and Seabiscuit responded. Eventually, the hard to handle, ill-tempered horse calmed down, and he returned to the easygoing, mild-mannered ways he enjoyed as a yearling. Eating and sleeping were his favorite pastimes. But, most of all, Seabiscuit loved to run. And he sure could run.

In the end, Seabiscuit was triumphant both off and on the racetrack. All in all, Seabiscuit competed in 89 races. He set 12 track records, often carrying the high weight of 130 to 132 pounds en route to 27 career stakes wins. He defeated the 1937 Triple Crown winner and Horse of the Year War Admiral in a match race, and capped off his career by winning the Santa Anita "Hundred Grander" handicap (fig. 10.4). Seabiscuit was the 1938 Horse of the Year, the Champion Handicap Division Horse in 1937 and 1938, and by the time of his retirement at the age of seven, Seabiscuit had become the all-time leading money earner with $437,730 (£282,000) in career earnings.

Today, it is easy to look back, scratch our head, and wonder what Howard and Smith were thinking, putting Seabiscuit through such a demanding schedule. Horses in training today rarely perform one-tenth of what Seabiscuit accomplished. However, in the end, history has proven to be the final judge in the soundness of their decision. A life-size bronze statue of Seabiscuit at Santa Anita Park in Arcadia, California, bears this tribute: "The main issue in life is not the victory but the fight; the essential thing is not to have won but to have fought well." Another statue

10.4 In the final race of his career, Seabiscuit, with jockey Red Pollard in the saddle, cruised to a one and one half-length victory in the "Hundred Grander" 1940 Santa Anita Handicap in California.

honors him at the Howard family's Ridge-wood Ranch (fig. 10.5). In 1958, Seabiscuit was inducted into the National Museum of Racing and Hall of Fame.

Seabiscuit's story has thrilled the hearts and minds of anyone who has ever dreamed of a better future. Indeed, millions were, and still are, entertained by his heroics, now detailed in several books, documentaries, and feature films. In fact, what I think is one of the greatest quotes pertaining to equine athletes and what they give to the world was written about Seabiscuit. In his book *Seabiscuit: The Saga of a Great Champion* (Westholme Publishing, 2004), B.K. Beck-with said:

10.5 In 2007, a statue of Seabiscuit was erected at the Howard family's Ridgewood Ranch were Seabiscuit is buried in a secret location. The Seabiscuit Heritage Foundation of Willits, California, continues to promote the memory and accomplishments of this famous racehorse.

There are countless millions of others who have won…who have found the world a little bit better place to live in because of a great horse…It is not so much what he has done in life that counts—the victories, the glorious defeats, the fabulous money earned. It is, in the final analysis, the kindly, courageous, honest manner in which he has lived…Thus will the fine flame of his soul burn in the tunnel of time forever.

Postscript

Not every horse can be a champion, a Seabiscuit. But every horse deserves to be treated like one. Each equine athlete deserves the same loving care and nurturing Seabiscuit received from his handlers so that he, too, can live up to his fullest potential—whatever it may be.

Throughout the ages, the horse has been man's constant companion. On more than one occasion, our very survival has depended on a trusty horse. We have looked to the horse to help us and entertain us with tasks both spectacular and mundane. If we wish to return the full measure of what the horse has given us, what he has contributed to our own evolution and happiness, then we must look beyond our world and do our utmost to provide opportunity for the horse to flourish. Our own goals can be met and our horses can be all they can be, if only we acknowledge and embrace the magic within them.

Photo Credits

- Courtesy of Kerry Thomas: 1.1, 1.3 A & B, 2.1 A, 3.1, 4.4, 6.1, 7.1, 9.5 B

- Courtesy of Larry Knepper: 1.2 A, 1.6 E, 7.5 A–C, 8.1 A & B

- Courtesy of the Carol M. Highsmith Archive, Library of Congress, Prints and Photographs Division: 1.2 B & C

- Courtesy of the Seabiscuit Heritage Foundation: 1.4 A, 10.1, 10.2, 10.3, 10.4, 10.5

- Courtesy of the Library of Congress, Prints and Photographs Division: 1.4 B & C, 1.6 A–D

- Courtesy of Gillian Vallis: 1.5 A & B, 1.6 G, 2.2 A & B, 2.3, 2.4 A–D, 2.5 A–E, 3.2, 3.3 A–H, 3.4 A–C, 4.1, 4.2, 4.5, 5.2, 5.3 A & B, 5.6, 6.2 A–K, 8.3 B, 8.6 A, 8.7 A–E, 9.1, 9.2, 9.3 A–C, 9.5 A

- Courtesy of the APHA/Kayla Starnes ©2011: 1.6 F, 8.6 B

- Courtesy of Steve Barger: 2.1 B, 4.3, 5.7 A–C

- Courtesy of Photosbyz.com: 2.6, 5.1 A & B, 5.4, 5.5, 7.2, 7.6, 7.7, 8.3 A, 8.4

- Courtesy of Amanda Duckworth: 4.6

- Courtesy of the APHA © 2011: 8.2

- Courtesy of Ovidiu Vajiala: 8.5, 8.8, 9.4

- Courtesy of Amanda Smith: 9.6 A–C

Index

Page numbers in *italics* indicate illustrations. Brown numbers refer to boxed text.